TEACH FOR TRANSFER

A Programed Book

MADELINE HUNTER, ED.D
Principal, University Elementary School
Lecturer, Graduate School of Education
University of California, Los Angeles
Educational Consultant

TIP PUBLICATIONS
El Segundo, California

THEORY INTO PRACTICE PUBLICATIONS

Motivation Theory for Teachers
Reinforcement Theory for Teachers
Retention Theory for Teachers
Teach More—Faster!
Teach for Transfer

Additional Publications

Aide-ing in Education
Prescription For Improved Instruction
Improving Your Child's Behavior
Parent-Teacher Conferencing
Mastery Teaching

Copyright, © 1971, by Madeline Hunter
TIP Publications
P.O. Box 514
El Segundo, California 90245

Twenty-third Printing, June, 1985
Twenty-Fourth Printing, October, 1985
Twenty-Fifth Printing, January, 1986
Twenty-Sixth Printing, August 1986
Twenty-Seventh Printing, September, 1987
Twenty-Eighth Printing, June, 1988

ISBN 0-935567-04-6

PRINTED IN THE UNITED STATES OF AMERICA

FOREWORD

Teach for Transfer, is the last book in this series which translates psychological principles into the language of the classroom. It is appropriately the final book, for "teaching for transfer" should be the end goal of all teaching. Using the same reasoning, it also should be the first goal of all teaching for the ability to transfer previous learnings to a new situation is the heart and core of all creativity, problem solving, and critical thinking.

The writer spent two years extracting from psychological research the principles of transfer which seemed useful and critical to daily teaching. The task was a herculean one and the temptation to abandon it was a nagging irritant to its completion. To the writer's knowledge, this is the first time such research has been pulled together in a format usable by teachers and consequently it may have serious omissions.

With feedback from reader usage plus field testing the usefulness and productivity of these transfer principles in our experimental school at UCLA, such a book could provide the basis of an educational design which produces the creative, responsible, self-actualizing, critical thinker of our educational dreams.

Madeline Hunter

To four educational "giants" who taught for transfer:

Dr. Ellen B. Sullivan who "turned me on" in psychology and saw that I developed professional rigor,

Dr. Evan Keisler who focused me on the relevance of psychology to education,

Dr. May Seagoe who helped me make that relevance explicit,

Dr. John I. Goodlad who made possible the demonstration of that relevance in reality,

this book is respectfully and gratefully dedicated.

TABLE OF CONTENTS

CHAPTER I

THE IMPORTANCE OF TRANSFER

Present day educators are firmly committed to an educational process which will result in creative endeavor, critical thinking, and effective problem solving by the learner.

The key to successful achievement of such learner behavior is provided by psychological research in *transfer of learning* for the core of creativity and problem solving is the student's ability to transfer past learnings to the creative solution of present problems. This ability to transfer past learning which is appropriate to a present situation is one of the most critical factors in perception, insight, reasoning and originality.

Like mushrooms, programs are sprouting all over the country, each purporting to develop such desirable behavior in the learner. These programs are focused on a "way" of conducting schooling (open structure, The British Infant School, new curriculum endeavors, etc.). Few programs, however, address themselves to the identification and deliberate incorporation of those factors which research has indicated contribute most importantly to creativity and problem solving. It is not the "way" of conducting schooling which guarantees success but whether there is conscious and deliberate inclusion of those factors which generate creative learner behavior. Like meals, educational programs cannot be judged by appearance or activities but must be evaluated in terms of the "educational nutrients" they contain which are particularly appropriate for each learner's optimal growth.

Regardless of any particular method or program, the planning of the teacher is probably the most critical element in generating the transfer which yields student productivity and creativity. This planning makes the difference between "hoping that it will happen" and "seeing that it does." It is so you as a teacher can incorporate the power of transfer in your daily classroom activities that this book has been written.

Transfer is not a new classroom phenomenon. Its results have long been a matter of concern to teachers. Why do students spell correctly on a test and then miss the same words in written work? Why can't beginning readers see that "come" and "Come" are the same word? Why do high school students write carefully in their English class but indecipherably on math papers? Why can they solve the problems in the math book but seem unable to figure out the average rainfall in geography?

These are some of the many questions that vex and perplex teachers as students possess knowledge and skills in one set of circumstances but do not apply those same skills to other situations that require them. We must develop ways to teach so a student can utilize his learning to solve new and different situations five minutes hence, tomorrow, next week, or in the remote future.

This ability to learn in one situation and then to use that learning, possibly in modified or generalized form in other situations where it is appropriate, is known as *transfer* of learning. The phenomenon of transfer of learning is fantastically important for two reasons:

1. Transfer is the heart and core of problem solving, creative thinking and all other higher mental processes as well as inventions and artistic products.

2. Transfer of learning provides a source of real economy of time and energy because, as previous learning facilitates or interferes with new learning, such transfer of learning can effectively decrease or seriously increase the time needed to achieve any new learning.

Transfer, however, does not always occur automatically or efficiently. *Significant and efficient transfer predictably occurs only if we teach to achieve it.* Such transfer is accurate generalization of learning to new situations and is sought as the end product of all formal instruction and schooling.

Transfer of learning is obvious with observable skills. A violinist can learn to play a cello much more quickly and easily than a flutist can. A linguist can learn a new language more quickly than a teacher of literature. A pilot can learn to fly a new plane more easily than a bus driver. A boy who has "tinkered" with his car can learn to change a carburetor much faster than his higher I.Q'd friend who has never lifted the hood. In each of these cases, the learner possesses some skills and knowledge which can transfer to and accelerate the new learning. Other learners must start more nearly from scratch. In fact, *the possession of learnings which can transfer is a much better predictor of successful new learning than is the age or I.Q. of the learner.*

Transfer of learning isn't always helpful. Sometimes the knowledge or skills already possessed by the learner interfere with acquiring new learning. If you learned to drive with an automatic transmission, it is difficult for you to remember to use the clutch in a car with a manual shift. If you learned to cook with gas, it is difficult for you not to burn the food when you first use an electric stove. If you are accustomed to backing a car without a trailer, it is difficult to remember to turn the wheel in the opposite direction when you have a trailer attached.

Transfer of learning is very evident in skills such as we have described. It is not so easily perceived, but transfer can be just as powerfully present to facilitate or impede a student's learning of those facts, concepts, processes, beliefs, attitudes, and interests for which we as teachers are responsible.

An example of such transfer is highly visible in foreign language learning. It is facilitating to meaning when similarities yield appropriate transfer such as "mucho" for "much," "non" for "no," "difficile" for "difficult," "ya" for "yes," "ambassadeur" for "ambassador." In the same way, inappropriate transfer from previous knowledge of the English order of words results in interference in learning when "white house" must be "casa blanca," "I have no" must be "no tengo."

Transfer also occurs with interests and attitudes as we find ourselves disliking a new person because he looks like someone who "gypped" us in the past or we reject a new food because it reminds us of something unpleasant.

Whenever old learnings assist the acquisition of new learning, we refer to this facilitation as *positive transfer*. When old learnings interfere with the acquisition of new learning, we refer to this interference as *negative transfer*. There is no argument among psychologists about the occurrence or importance of transfer. The essential question is how teachers can best utilize transfer to increase learning. It is essential to efficiency in the teaching-learning process that we encourage as much positive transfer as possible and minimize or eliminate any negative transfer that might give us "educational static."

How can we produce the efficiency and economy of learning that result from transfer? First, we must identify the factors that generate transfer, either positive or negative. Second, we must learn to recognize those factors in an instructional situation. Third, as we plan and teach we must take those factors into account so they work to the advantage of the learner.

In this book we will describe the important factors that operate to encourage or discourage transfer of learning. We will present examples of how you might use each factor to advantage in teaching, and then we will ask you a question to see how successful we have been in our presentation. You will select an answer and turn to the page indicated. On that page you will be told if you are correct and directed to the next learning. If your answer is not correct, you will be told why and be directed back to the question so you may select a better asnwer. Let's see how well we have done so far.

Transfer of learning refers to:

a. Moving learning from one place to another. . . . .
. . . . Turn to page 5, top

b. The translation of one skill to another skill. . . . .
. . . . Turn to page 5, bottom

c. Changing a learning. . . . . Turn to page 6, top.

d. Previous learning influencing the acquisition of new learning.
. . . . Turn to page 6, bottom

a. You said transfer of learning refers to moving learning from one place to another.

In a way you're right. However, we do not actually move a learning for it still "remains" where it was originally learned. It can also be "present," however, in the new learning. Turn back to the question on page 4 and select an answer which indicates the influence of the already possessed learning on the new learning that is to be acquired.

b. You said transfer of learning refers to the translation of one skill to another skill.

In a way you're right. However, rather than being translated or changed from one learning to another, transfer of learning refers to the fact that the knowledge or skills you already possess can assist or hinder you when you learn something new. Turn back to the question on page 4 and select an answer that implies this influence.

c. You said transfer of learning refers to changing learning.

The learning is not necessarily changed. It may remain in the identical state. Transfer refers to the fact that the degree of difficulty encountered in acquiring a new learning may be influenced (made harder or easier) by the presence of old learnings. Turn back to the question on page 4 and select an answer that reflects this influence.

d. You said transfer of learning refers to previous learning influencing the acquisition of new learning.

Right you are! (Positive reinforcement! We want to increase the probability that you will continue to select the right answers. If you don't understand what we're talking about, you should read the book *Reinforcement Theory* from this same series). Whenever old learning makes the acquisition of a new learning easier, it is positively transferring to the new learning. When an old learning makes a new learning more difficult to achieve, it is negatively transferring. We hope that what you learn from this book will positively transfer to your teaching to make each day in the classroom easier and more successful. Turn to page 7 so we can start that positive transfer.

Factors which generate transfer

As we plan for each day's teaching, we need to consider four important factors that generate transfer. Those factors can increase the effiiciency and economy achieved when an old learning positively transfers and thereby facilitates new learning. These same four factors can also produce negative transfer and operate to the students' detriment. In a way, transfer is like a powerful drug. It can be productive or destructive. Knowing its power, we can use transfer to facilitate learning. At those times when we do *not* want the old learning to transfer because it will interfere with the acquisition of the new learning we can learn how to minimize or eliminate that negative transfer.

No one of these four factors which generates transfer is the most powerful. The potency of each factor changes in relation to a particular learning situation so we must constantly be aware (or beware!) of the presence of all of them.

What do you think those four key factors are that encourage a past learning to transfer into a present or future situation? Jot them down so, after reading this book, you can check to see which ones you already knew and which new factors you have learned. By doing this you should develop a "set" or motivation to identify and label those factors, therefore they will be made likely to transfer into your future teaching with an increase in students' learning that will really amaze you.

Four factors which generate transfer are:

1. _____

2. _____

3. _____

4. _____

Which of these four do you think is the most important to always incorporate in your teaching? Why?

_____

_____

_____

_____

To the next page.

Very simply stated, the four factors which generate transfer, *either* positive or negative, are:

I. The similarity of the situation in which something is learned and the situation to which that learning may transfer.

II. The student's association of the old and new learnings for any one of many reasons.

III. The degree of effectiveness ot the original learning.

IV. The perception of essential or unvarying elements which exist in both the old and the new learnings.

These four factors can operate in any learning situation, and seldom is only one of them having an effect. In this book we will deal with each one separately to become familiar with it. In the same way we study separately the circulatory system and the digestive system of the human body knowing they are always operating in relationship one to the other. Often, however, the physician can adjust only one system and restore health. In like manner we can focus on one factor in transfer and produce efficient and productive learning.

Let's examine each of these four factors in detail and learn how we can utilize that factor in the classroom to facilitate the acquisition of new learning, to accelerate the solution of problems, and to generate creativity in ideas and products.

CHAPTER II

SIMILARITY OF TWO LEARNINGS

Transfer is generated by the similarity of the situation in which something is learned and the situation to which that learning may transfer.

A factor which must be considered in every lesson is the similarity of the situation in which something is learned and the situation to which we wish that learning to transfer. The more similar the two situations, the more learning will transfer or "spill over" from one to the other. For example, we are more apt to make the mistake of using our friend's name for her twin sister than for her older or younger sister.

Knowing that similarity generates transfer, if we want to encourage or maximize transfer we should make the two learning situations as similar as possible. When we want to discourage transfer because the old learning will interfere with the new learning, we should make the two learning situations as different as possible.

Let's look at some familiar examples. Usually students wear their best clothes on important occasions when their behavior must be exemplary such as church, going out for dinner, weddings, or important visits and trips. Knowing this, we may encourage students to "dress up" for school parties and dances so the similarity of wearing their best clothes will transfer their "company" manners from one situation to their good behavior in another.

Conversely, when youth groups use school auditoriums, if the lay leaders allow running, yelling, and disorderly behavior inappropriate to school, we often (to our dismay) find that disorderly behavior transferring to school assemblies.

Another common instance of transfer with similarity of situation occurs as our response when picking up a phone generalizes so at home we answer with the name of our school and at school where a more formal response is required the informal "hi" sometimes slips out. This same phenomenon of response generalization due to similarity is apparent when the young child calls his teacher "mamma" or

11

the teacher snags her hose on a classroom chair and an inappropriate (at school) expletive slips out.

Possibilities for Producing Similarities

Every day in classroom this potent factor of perceived similarity of two situations operates to the advantage or detriment of learning. When it will facilitate learning, there are many ways we, as teachers, can encourage the *perception* of similarity in two learning situations and thereby encourage positive transfer. That similarity can exist in:

A. Factors in the environment (objects, people, sounds, time, etc.)

B. Factors within the student (feelings, motivation, set to perform)

C. Factors in the activity of the student (the method of learning or utilization of a particular sensory mode)

In other words, the similarity of (a) what a student *perceives* in the environment, (b) how he *feels* and *thinks,* and (c) what he *does* can all generate transfer from a past learning situation to a present or future one.

These possibilities for producing similarity are not mutually exclusive. It may be more effective, however, to place major emphasis or effort on one possibility rather than another. In the following pages we will consider each possibility separately to develop ways we might utilize it to maximize transfer so old learning will facilitate the acquisition of new learning. We also need to be alert to the necessity for using these possibilities to minimize transfer if the old learning will interfere with the acquisition of new learning.

A. Similarity of Elements in the Environment

Behavior learned in one environment tends to transfer to other environments that are similar. The quiet behavior learned in the library will be more apt to transfer to other rooms with study tables and books than to the gymnasium or cafeteria. If disorderly behavior is permitted in one classroom, it may transfer to another classroom because the environments are perceived as the same by the student. As a result the second teacher will have to spend more time on control.

Usually we cannot replicate the entire environment when we wish learning to transfer, nor change the environment completely when we wish to eliminate transfer, but we can more nearly achieve either outcome by intentionally arranging certain key factors in that environment and focusing the student's attention on those critical factors. For example, despite a multitude of differences, the presence of the same teacher can cause the acceptable behavior of the classroom to transfer to the school bus or to the playground while without the key factor of that teacher completely different (and possibly unacceptable) behavior might emerge.

The importance of such key factors in making two situations similar is obvious. We all have observed that regardless of the differentness of the rest of the environment, passing out tests will cause a mental set (be it anxiety or confidence) to transfer to any testing situation. In similar manner, the auditory stimulus of the fire alarm signal should produce trained drill behavior by the student regardless of where in the geography of the school he happens to be when he hears it. We teach so that his learned behavior transfers to any situation where there is the critical element (the sound of the alarm) that is similar.

To facilitate desirable transfer, the important job of the teacher is to help learners identify and verbally label ("Whenever you hear the alarm you will need to") the essential and key environmental clue which signals the similarity of the situation so the appropriate action occurs rather than taking the chance that students may focus on unimportant or nonsignificant elements. In our examples, it is the presence of books, test blanks, or the alarm which constitutes the essential cue that triggers the transfer of learning and behavior from a past situation to a current one, not all of the countless other possibly vivid but unimportant factors.

Changing those key factors in the environment and *calling that change to the attention of the learner* will minimize transfer for it will signal him that he needs to behave differently, that this is *not* the same situation. By this technique we are able to avoid undesirable transfer which could otherwise occur. For example, a teacher might call to the attention of the students that *no names will be placed on these tests*, they are "merely for survey purposes" thus changing the factor of identification of each test in order to reduce the transfer of anxiety or competitive factors which could operate to influence a different kind of test situation.

An all too common example of transfer occurring from similarity of environment is the well documented observation that when there is a problem in the classroom, the teacher's behavior to solve that problem will probably reflect what happened to him in school when he was that age, rather than the content of his courses in teacher education which were designed to guide his professional behavior. The cause is probably that his present classroom problem situation is perceived as more similar to his own pre-collegiate classroom experience than it is to his university classroom of adults. Consequently, the knowledge of what his own teacher did under similar conditions, transfers (often inappropriately) to the present situation. As a result, we may find a teacher having students write "I will not - - - - - -" a hundred times. We may see teachers giving an unmotivated student an "F," or piling on useless homework when, in their professional training, teachers have learned more productive ways of dealing with such problems. Unfortunately, too often the college courses are not at all similar to the real world of teaching so that desirable learning and behavior are not transferring into the classroom situation.

We have cited only a few examples of how a present environment can be perceived as similar to a past environment by the learner. He may be responding to the similarity of the objects, people, sounds, time, or any one of an infinite number of possibilities. We need to examine each possibility in the environment, *emphasizing and labeling the key factor of similarity* if we wish to encourage transfer. We must minimize or eliminate that similarity if we do not wish transfer to occur because it would interfere with present learning.

Now let's examine another possibility of similarity that would produce transfer—the student's way of thinking or feeling as he is approaching or working on the learning task.

B. Factors Within the Student—The Same Feelings, Motivation, or Set to Perform.

Similarity of Emotions or Feeling.

The factor of emotions in transfer becomes highly visible in our former example of passing out tests and illustrates the way many factors which promote transfer interact in the same situation, i.e., the presence of the tests (environmental), the set to perform in an examination (thinking), and the emotion (feeling), which is generated by being evaluated. Groans and anxiety attacks transfer from past situations to the present one for those students who have experienced difficulty in the past. This is such a common phonemenon that "test anxiety" negatively transfers, interferes with performance, and results in students failing even though they possess the knowledge and the required competency. We all have had the experience of being unable to remember a familiar name or phone number when we are under stress. Conversely, previous feelings of success and adequacy in test taking can transfer and enable students to perform at a level higher than their typical performance. This latter phenomenon is highly visible as athletes in competition break previous records.

Equally familiar are those feelings that negatively transfer such as "I don't get it, I never did understand math" which interfere with a student even attempting to understand algebra. The feeling of "I really enjoy working with my hands" positively transfers and propels activities requiring manual dexterity, while "I'm a bumble fingers" transfers and results in a half-hearted attempt. Learning to avoid a difficult task by feigning illness will transfer into a completely new situation where the person experiences the same feelings of difficulty or inadequacy. Psychosomatic ills are often the result of a person perceiving (possibly subconsciously) a current situation as similar to one in the past that "made him sick."

Emotions are such powerful factors in learning that we need to be ever watchful to avoid negative transfer from unpleasant feeling tones. All of us wish to avoid unpleasant situations. Consequently, we transfer the feeling of "get me away from this" to any situation we don't like. When an unsuccessful student experiences failure, he may "get himself away from it" by avoiding that subject in the future or even dropping out of school. Making school a pleasant place where the student achieves success should transfer to his approaching new learning opportunities with enthusiasm. Developing a "zest" for learning is a highly desirable teaching objective for that feeling can transfer to and propel all future learning situations.

The verbal mediation of labeling an enjoyable situation, "This is fun, isn't it?" should transfer "approach" behavior to new situations when that situation is similarly labeled by, "This is going to be fun!" or "This is like the assignment you enjoyed so much last week."

Labeling an emotion is helpful because it brings awareness of a feeling to a conscious level. Then the learner has the opportunity to acknowledge and deal with that feeling. The teacher without becoming an analyst can matter of factly state, "I can see you're angry but—" or "You may be worried about it however—" or "I think you're having such a good time because—" or "I know you're disappointed so—." Often such labeling helps separate the emotions from the situation so each can be dealt with productively and any transfer to future situations will be positive. We will learn more about the transfer of emotions later in this book when we look at the association of two learnings.

Along with his feelings, the way a student is thinking or his intentions in learning can cause him to perceive a present situation as similar to one he has experienced in the past. We call this factor, *set to perform.*

Similarity of Motivation or Set to Perform.

"Let's see if you can answer this detective question," usually elicits from the learner a mental set to look for inferences rather than to recall memorized facts and he will more likely seek clues which will guide him to the answer. Consequently, his "deducing" behavior will be more apt to transfer to his attack on the current problem than if you stimulate his response by "Who knows the answer to this question?" The latter stimulus will more likely result in a mental set to comb his memory files for the correct remembered information.

A vivid demonstration of transfer of "set" can be observed if you ask a student to complete "Bob had a dog. Mary had a_____." In most cases you can accurately predict that transfer from past learnings will produce "cat" as the answer. By changing the "set to perform" to nursery rhymes you can almost guarantee a different type of

16

response will transfer into the answer. Try stimulating his response by "Hickory dickory dock, the mouse ran up the clock," Mary had a_____." We'll bet you'll get "little lamb." Powerful, isn't it?

Another example of this set to perform can be seen by saying to a group of learners "5-10-15-20-, 2-4-6-8_____." In almost every case you'll get "10" as the response. If, however, you generate transfer from a different set by "Let's give a cheer for Bill, 2-4-6-8_____" "Who do we appreciate?" will be the more likely response.

Dividing students into teams causes them to perceive the present situation as similar to past team situations. Consequently, this perceived similarity will elicit the set for competitive behavior between teams and (hopefully) cooperative behavior within a team. If you wish to elicit from your students only cooperative behavior and minimize competitive behavior, you need to eliminate the similarity of the present situation to previous situations where the set to perform has been competitive. Making comparisons of different student's performance often yields undesired transfer because comparisons have been previously associated with competition and the "I'm going to be best" syndrome. We naively say to a student "It doesn't make any difference what grade someone else gets" when grading itself is usually based on comparative and therefore competitive performance.

When we introduce a competitive situation to a student, we need to anticipate which set to perform will transfer from past competition into the present learning. Some of the possibilities are:

1) "I'll never win so there's no point in trying."

2) "I'll bet I can win!"

3) "I cheated last time and didn't get caught."

4) "If I really work at it I can make it."

Depending on what each has learned from past competitive situations, students will transfer different learnings into the present situation. Obviously some of these learnings will enhance effort while others are debilitating. A teacher needs to estimate whether positive or negative transfer will occur when competition is present so unanticipated negative transfer does not interfere with present learning.

The propelling power of mental set has been illustrated by one research project that demonstrated brain damaged and slow learners who had transferred an appropriate set, learned faster than normal learners who had not developed that set and consequently could not transfer it to facilitate learning.

Let's try some first-hand experience with this *set to perform* as you become a learner and do this problem in addition.

"A bus left the depot with five passengers and the driver. At the first stop it picked up six more passengers. At the next stop seven more got on. (Are you adding?) At the next stop three passengers got off and only one got on. The following stop added six more passengers. The next stop added nine new passengers but four of the previous passengers got off. At the stop just before the end of the line nine passengers got off. If you have been doing your addition accurately, you have the answer to our question: "How many times did the bus stop?"

If you are like most readers, your typical set to deal with *all* the numbers in a problem transferred into your present behavior and you were adding and subtracting (in spite of the instruction that this was a problem in addition). Your *set* from past experience negatively transferred and interfered with present performance.

Many classroom errors result from the same inappropriate transfer of "set to perform." It is difficult to teach openness to different points of view because students have learned the "one right answer" set. People with the set that "art should be representational" have a difficult time enjoying or appreciating abstract or nonrepresentational art. Students who have the set that "'we will learn the answer from the teacher" flounder when they are expected to discover those answers on their own. Conversely, students who believe they must discover everything, inappropriately transfer that behavior to situations where it is impossible for them to "discover" before they have learned some fundamentals in the field. (The author worked with a group of graduate students whose set to "discover through discussion" inappropriately transferred into their desire to "discover" all the principles of learning for themselves without reference to the years of work done by competent psychologists).

Teachers work hard to develop in their students a pervasive set to make decisions democratically. This set, too, can transfer inappro-

18

priately to decisions that should be made on a different basis. A first grade teacher was faced with this transfer of inappropriate set when a child brought a kitten to class. The children discussed its color, personality, similarity to other cats and the inevitable question arose, "Is it a boy kitten or a girl kitten?"

"How would we find out?" queried the teacher.

"Let's vote," decided the first graders.

It is obvious there is no "right" or "wrong" set to perform until the learning situation is described. The set to "listen to directions" will yield positive transfer in a fire drill but negative transfer when the learning task demands the learner think for himself. An innovative set transfers positively into creative endeavor but interferes with learning the correct spelling or pronunciation of a word.

Helping the student identify and select from his past learning the set which will yield the appropriate propulsion to present learning is the hallmark of a successful teacher. The introduction to any lesson should include focusing the student on the learning to be accomplished and the identification of his own appropriate "set to perform" thereby increasing the probability that he will select a set from the repertoire he has developed in previous learnings which will yield positive transfer to his current endeavor. It is educationally economical that we take time to introduce or identify with students the appropriate set so an inappropriate one does not transfer to and interfere with a present learning situation. (Remember the bus "addition" problem?)

When we are trying to prevent a previous set from transferring to a new situation where it would be inappropriate, we must do something to make the current situation *perceivably* different from past situations where that particular set was appropriate. For example, in learning to solve word problems, it is very difficult for students to change their set from computing the right answer to a set for dealing with the important and essential elements of (1) identifying the question that is asked, (2) seeking the numerical data that are relevant in answering that question (what numbers will we use?), and (3) determining the operation to perform with those numbers (what will we do with those facts?). To eliminate the computational set ("figure out

19

the answer"), we must make the present situation perceivably different from past situations where the assignment was to compute the answer. We do this by changing key elements in the situation so we get thinking behavior instead of headlong (and often heedless) computation. To accomplish this change of set, we might present a problem where no numbers are given so it will be impossible for the students' computational set to transfer. We can work with word problems such as "Tom had a certain number of pages of homework to do. He had a limited number of hours to complete the homework. How would we find out how many pages he must do each hour if he is to finish?" The result will be development of an equation or plan for solving the problem rather than a computational project.

For too many students, unfortunately, school is a place where you do not consider all possibilities but must learn only right answers. Consequently, that one-right-answer set transfers into situations where it is inappropriate because there can be several "right" answers. As a result, the more desirable behavior of seeking alternative solutions stops as soon as the first solution is offered and accepted. In fact, even a nod from the teacher can trigger the "that's-all" syndrome. Conversely, a response from the teacher of "Why do you think that?" or "Who has a different idea?" can, by association with a previous experience, transfer the "oops, I'm wrong" feeling and the student may abandon his idea even if it was correct. To avoid this negative transfer, the teacher may need to confirm the student's response by "That's a good idea" before pushing his thinking further with "Why do you think that?" In the same way the teacher may need to respond with "That's one good suggestion" but continue asking "Who has a different idea?"

Again, evoking the appropriate set by stating, "There's no one best way to solve this problem" or "There are many possibilities, let's list some" should transfer from the students' past experience the mental set to seek alternative possibilities and many solutions. Students who have experienced only "find the one right answer" have no past set (considering many alternatives) to transfer into the present situation and the teacher must first teach the behavior of seeking alternatives before that behavior can transfer into other situations where it is appropriate.

Unfortunately in the profession of teaching, we too suffer from this same "one right answer" syndrome which inappropriately transfers and results in our seeking THE one solution to our learning problems. (THE best method for teaching reading or THE best style of teaching or that "perceptual motor training will eliminate reading failures." Does it sound familiar?). This set would be appropriate if there *were* one best way, but unfortunately there are so many variables in teaching that all decisions must take into account "in this particular set of circumstances" and like so many other things in life, solutions vary when circumstances vary.

Continual focus on the set of *"under what conditions would this work"* should yield positive transfer and do much to prevent teachers seeking one fail-proof program to be administered in equal dosage to all learners in the same way that the diagnostic and prescriptive set of a doctor avoids a patent medicine or identical prescription for all patients.

We have discussed a student's perceiving one situation as similar to another because it (1) contained the same elements in the environment or because (2) he experienced the same feelings or set to perform. A third factor which will influence his perception of two learning situations as similar is what he is doing, the sensory modality he is using, or his method of learning.

C. Similarity of the Activity of the Learner

Similarity of Sensory Mode (vision, hearing, tactile, etc.).

Knowledge about one thing can transfer to another if one of our sensory modes perceives it as the same and sends us the same signal. In most cases, this transfer promotes highly effective and efficient learning; however, an inappropriate signal of similarity from one of our senses can cause us to err. Students confuse "their" and "there" because they sound the same. You can't tell how to pronounce "read" until you know how it is used (i.e., "read the book" or "the book was read") because the visual stimulus is the same. Most of us cannot distinguish synthetic from natural fabrics by appearance, but must "feel" them.

Suppose we wished our students to "discover" the relationships involved in balancing a teeter totter. They would need to perceive

21

the relationship between the weight and the distance of that weight from the fulcrum. We would give the learners the materials for experimentation and, knowing that guided discovery produces more efficient and effective learning and more transfer than merely "turning the students loose," we might have them record their data in this manner:

Left side		fulcrum	Right side	
weight	distance		weight	distance
1	3		3	1
1	5		5	1

By having learners record their observations in this fashion, we would guide the students into focusing on visual cues which reveal the quantative relationships.

When we wished to aid the transfer of the discovery of ratios or numerical relationships to other situations where such relationships exist (such as the ratio of the speed of a car to the distance required for stopping), we can facilitate that transfer by having the students record data on the same type of chart. The similarity of displaying data in the two situations should trigger students' seeking the presence of predictable quantative relationships without the teacher needing to suggest that those relationships exist.

Again, we need to remind you that these categories of similarity are not mutually exclusive. This example of similarity of sensory mode might also have been cited under similarity of mode of attack.

Similarity of Method of Teaching or Learning.

What we *do* when we teach or what we expect students to *do* to learn may cause them to perceive situations as similar so the learning in one situation transfers to the other.

When they are reading, we teach students to take notes for subsequent study or for use in discussion and written work. Then, we bring an outstanding speaker into the classroom to make an important presentation while, to our dismay, students listen unmindful of the usefulness of recording main points or pertinent ideas when those ideas are presented verbally.

If we wish our students' note-taking skill to transfer into recording from a speaker's input, we can trigger this transfer by seeing that they have paper and pencil in hand (same objects in environment). We can also train them to take notes (same method of learning) from auditory input (same modality) so the situational similarity of the sound of a speaker's voice will evoke the learning strategy of recording main points.

Again, we need to remind you that we are merely citing examples, not presenting an exhaustive analysis of each category of similarity. Don't worry if you can't precisely identify one category from the other. Unlimited possibilities for eliciting transfer exist in every learning situation. We have separated these categories of similarity to encourage you, as a creative teacher, to look beyond the more obvious ones. By doing this you will discover the power of the more subtle factors of similarity which contribute to transfer so you can use those factors to develop classroom opportunities for accelerated learning. We have discussed the similarity of the sensory mode and the method of teaching or learning. Now let's examine a third possibility for similarity of learning behavior.

Similarity of General Principles or Mode of Attack.

The game of "twenty questions" gives us a common example of the development of a particular mode of attack which uses the same general principles in finding the correct answer. First, the participants identify the category in which the answer belongs and then narrow that category by asking questions about sub-categories until they locate the precise area in which the answer resides. Once this mode of attack is developed, its transfer into each new question makes the performers so efficient it seems as if they have extrasensory perception or are "intuiting" the answer.

Once the "decision making" mode of attack is learned, the ability to (1) specify the problem to be solved, (2) identify possible alternative solutions, (3) anticipate the consequences of each, and then (4) select the best solution, should transfer to all situations which require decision making. As a result, we should not expect intelligent decision making to alternate with "coin flipping" in circumstances which require the former behavior. Teaching for the transfer of considered judgment and intelligent problem solving rather than guessing or waiting for divine revelation is certainly an important educational objective and one which this book was written to help you achieve as you focus on the learning problems in your own classroom.

The general mode of attack for a scientist who wishes to solve a problem is (1) the observation of physical phenomena, (2) development of a hypothesis, and (3) the designing of an experiment to test it. On the other hand, one of the most important sources of data for the psychiatrist is the identification of feelings and their effect on behavior. Consequently, when either professional "hits a snag," transfer of mode of attack causes the scientist to look for observable physical data while the psychiatrist seeks inferential or interpretive cues in human behavior.

The story is told of a party hostess who passed a tray of expensive pastries; however, her sharp glance told her husband not to take any.

"She must be running out of pastries," thought a guest who was a restaurateur.

"He must have high cholesterol," thought a doctor.

"He must be reducing," thought a woman who was overweight.

"She must be saving money by not ordering them for the family," thought an economical guest.

Each was transferring past learning to his interpretation of the present situation.

The relevance of this story to teaching is that we must constantly keep in mind that different interpretations or student behaviors often reflect the transfer of differing past learning to a common present situation.

We should strive to develop in our students a pervasive mode of attack which is directed toward seeking the relationships, generalizations, and classification systems which make learning meaningful rather than the frantic "I-hope-I-can-remember-the-facts" set which is all too common. The former set would result in understanding cause-effect relationships in history, the latter in memorizing names and dates.

After reading this book (and others in this series), we hope that using learning theory to solve instructional problems will become your mode of attack (rather than falling back on educational recipes and platitudes) and this skill will transfer to your daily planning and teaching performance.

We have given brief examples of the factors which can make two learning situations appear to be similar. Those factors exist:

A. In the environment (objects, people, sounds, time, etc.)

B. Within the learner (feelings, motivation, set to perform)

C. In what the learner is doing (sensory mode utilized, method of learning)

Don't worry if you cannot clearly discern whether an example falls in one category or another. They are not that discrete. Just remember to look for sources of possible similarity between two learning situations. Encourage students to identify and label them or *create perceivable similarities* if you wish learning from one situation to transfer to the other. This transfer is enormously expedited if the learner discovers or, when necessary, the teacher points out the similar elements. In this way the learner will focus on the significant clues which generate appropriate transfer rather than extraneous ones which get him nowhere or even may interfere.

In cases of "discovery" learning, research indicates that guidance by the teacher to see that the student makes the discovery, (*not* telling the answer) facilitates learning and also increases the probability of that learning transferring more effectively into new situations. This teacher guidance should take the form of behavior or questions which focus the student on key elements, alert him to significant relationships, and evoke the seeking and verbalization of generalizations. Surprisingly, the more effective guidance a teacher gives (again this is stimulating the learner to accomplish the learning, *not* showing or giving him the answer) the more the student's discovery will yield positive transfer into new learnings. The more difficult the new learning, the more obviously effective is this transfer from *guided* discovery rather than turning students out to "academic pasture" and hoping they will discover. Occasionally, one hears the admonition "turn learning over to the students and get out of their way." In the author's opinion, this is an abdication of professional responsibility for teaching. We know that a teacher can facilitate learning even if it is "discovery" and the purpose of the teaching process is to make more probable the accomplishment of that learning. One should not expect students to discover unaided, the principles in math, language, and science that it has taken the best scholars throughout the ages to develop.

To increase positive transfer we should specify and label the similar elements ("How is what we're doing today the same as what we did last week?") and thereby insure students' focus on the presence of that element. By so doing, we deliberately encourage the perception of similarity that might not have occurred without our labeling action.

When transfer of old learning will interfere with a new learning, we can avoid that transfer by keeping the situations as different as possible, stressing the *differences* rather than the similarities. For example, we might say, "Today we will be doing something very different in our ball game. As each play is made the visiting coach will be talking over the loud speaker to point out the correct and incorrect aspects of the play. We will need to be listening carefully so we can not talk or shout to each other as we usually do in a game."

These directions stress the differentness of the present game situation from games in the past so the boisterous noise and customary visual focus are not so likely to transfer into the new situation where the players' auditory focus becomes more important.

Let's apply what we have learned about the similarity of two situations. The establishment of certain routines in the classroom is considered to be important in increasing efficiency of learning. Why do you think this is so?

a. Routine saves time .... Turn to page 27, top

b. Students know what to do .... Turn to page 27, bottom

c. Routine increases transfer .... Turn to page 28, top

d. Routine makes everyone more comfortable. ....
.... Turn to page 28, bottom

a. You said routine saves time.

That it does, but why? What is there about doing things the same way at the same time that can make learning more efficient? Turn back to the question on page 26 and select an answer that will explain why establishing certain routines save time.

b. You said routine was important because students know what to do.

And what a blessing that is! A routine means you are not starting from "scratch" with each new lesson, but think why it is that you do not want to start anew every period of every day. We all have some lessons which we would like to pretend never happened, blot out, and start afresh. Why is it you don't want that fresh antiseptic beginning every day? Turn back to the question on page 26 and select an answer that will explain why the same way of behaving in the same environment has learning advantages.

c. You said routine increases transfer.

It surely does! The same thing, the same time, the same way, in the same place provides maximum similarity of environment and therefore ensures a great deal of transfer. We would hope this transfer was desirable: students ready to learn (set to perform, mode of attack) with their materials ready (objects for teaching and learning) watching, listening, or working (sensory mode, methods of learning) and with enthusiasm from their previous success making them "hardly able to wait" (emotions and feelings).

Yes, routine certainly increases transfer of mental set, emotions, and behavior so routine can facilitate learning. Beware of those same routines if you wish to discourage transfer. If yesterday's lesson was a dabacle, MAKE TODAY DIFFERENT! If handwriting has approached the Sanscrit level, MAKE A CHANGE! If social studies is not going well, VARY THE WHOLE ROUTINE! If a student is experiencing frustration, failure, or boredom, don't let undesirable negative transfer, which could result from similarity of the environment, sink your educational operation.

Selecting this answer indicates you know that routine is one of many facets of similarity of environment and is desirable when we wish to elicit transfer of learning. When we do *not* wish transfer because it will impede learning, *change* the environment that surrounds that learning so you reduce or eliminate transfer. Now turn to page 29.

d. You said routine makes everyone more comfortable.

This must be true for you, or you would not have selected this answer. For other personalities, routine can become something to be avoided. Granted a certain amount of predictability in our environment is necessary for each of us to function, we need to raise the question, "Why do we function more efficiently when certain things remain the same?" Turn back to the question on page 26 and select an answer that will explain the desirability of a certain amount of that "sameness."

28

Achieving Similarity by Simulation

Simulation is the synthesis of as many factors as possible that will make a present learning situation similar to a future situation to which that learning is to transfer. An outstanding example of successful transfer of this kind was the first moon landing. The author visited N.A.S.A. in Houston before the "man-on-the-moon" project. The astronauts were being trained in docking and other procedures in simulation situations which were as similar as possible to anticipated future experience on the moon. The astronauts knew they were on the earth, that there was no danger, that the mechanisms were suspended in a hanger, and conditions of darkness, weightlessness, and movement were artificial. Yet under conditions where the key elements of similarity to a future situation were emphasized, this "on the earth" learning transferred successfully to a situation which no human being had previously encountered. The results of such simulation are a never to be forgotten testimonial to transfer theory and the power of its application in learning situations to insure successful future performance. Many school situations, which of necessity can not be real, can likewise be taught for successful transfer to real life and future performance.

Simulation of reality can be produced in the classroom by "let's pretend" or role playing situations where factors are arranged to produce maximum similarity to the future situations where the learning is to transfer. Examples of such simulation are practicing telephone etiquette with a real telephone and someone at the other end of the line, introductions with two people coming face to face, applying scientific method when there is a real problem to which the answer is not known rather than the all too common replication of an experiment where the answer is already known so the behavior being practiced is merely an exercise in following directions. (At what temperature does water boil? Most students know the answer is 212°F. If their thermometer reads 214°F, they will ignore the observed data and substitute the predetermined answer, a behavior antithetical to true scientific inquiry).

Using real problems in school rather than "book problems" is another example of valid simulation to encourage transfer to problem solving outside of school. "How will we decide what game to play?",

"What is a fair way to determine who goes first?", "Which decisions should the class make and which decisions are the teacher's?", and "What would be a fair test of what you have learned?", are a few of innumerable possibilities to provide experiences which parallel out of school reality and therefore encourage transfer of appropriate problem solving and decision making behavior to future situations throughout life.

Conversely, labeling as "decision making" behavior which is guessing the answer that is in someone else's mind such as "What safety rules shall we have in our halls?" or "What would you like to study?" (when the teacher has already decided) will result in transferring the behavior of "psyching out" what is in the teacher's mind rather than independent and intelligent decision making.

Practice the skill in the way it will be used is an important admonition to teachers. Role playing the resolution of a fight or argument using words instead of fists will provide a student with a repertoire of appropriate behaviors which he can then transfer to future conflict situation. While it is not a "cure all," such simulation is infinitely more effective than all the admonitions or "commercials" against fighting with which students are deluged.

Practicing behavior in the way it is going to be used is the common name for simulation. The transfer value of such practice cannot be over-emphasized. We should give learners the opportunity to consider the arguments of both sides before they vote in a school election, so that behavior of weighing alternatives will transfer to adult life, and critical thinking rather than prejudice can transfer into their future voting behavior. After learning throwing and catching skills, we need to systematically practice them in a game where "on your feet" decision making and dealing with the unanticipated are the essential elements which will transfer those skills into all sports. Unfortunately, "read the chapter and answer the questions at the end" is not a simulation of situations where critical reading is important, consequently a student may be able to do a school assignment with "A" quality yet read newspapers and periodicals with "F" comprehension and "Z" critical thinking.

The teaching of spelling is an outstanding example of lack of simulation of reality. For example, we wish the results from our instruction in spelling to transfer into the learner's written composition. Spelling, however, is often taught through lists dictated by a teacher. This is in no way a simulation of a future situation which requires correct spelling. Written composition is dissimilar to a spelling dictation situation so we often find little transfer of correct spelling. The words spelled correctly in the test are misspelled in the subsequent creative story or poem. In order to teach spelling so skills will transfer we must make the two learning situations more alike. Selecting words used in written expression, and testing for accuracy by dictation of a sentence so the student has to remember the whole sentence and write it as it generates from his own mind rather than from the teacher's voice, will make the spelling situation more similar to creative writing. The skills involved (correct spelling, capitals, and punctuation) will be more likely to transfer. Obviously, this is not the only factor necessary to produce good spellers but it is one way of utilizing the power of transfer to assist this vexing problem.

How would you simulate reality in this situation?:

Having taught the difference between fact and opinion, to give your students practice would you have them:

a. Read a story and distinguish fact from opinion?............
......................................Turn to page 32, top

b. Write five facts and five opinions?... Turn to page 32, bottom

c. Read a newspaper article and distinguish fact from opinion?
......................................Turn to page 33, top

d. Identify fact and opinion from statements on a test? ....
..................................Turn to page 33, bottom

a. You said you would have them read a story and distinguish fact from opinion.

You have the wisdom to see that students practice their skill but are you maximizing the transfer potential of such learning? Often stories should be enjoyed with little concern for facts and opinions. Turn back to the question on page 31 and select an answer that will be more apt to encourage transfer to future situations where that skill should be used.

b. You said you would have them write five facts and five opinions.

You are wise to get active participation from your learners rather than just "giving them the word" and hoping it transfers to situations where the skill is needed. Nevertheless they may merely recall previous learnings and not be applying the skill of discriminating. Turn back to the question on page 31 and select an answer which will reflect your reading about similarity of the situation in which something is learned and the future situation to which that learning should transfer.

c. **You said you would have them read a newspaper article and distinguish fact from opinion.**

Would that all teachers were as astute! You are making the situation in which something is learned as similar as possible to future situations to which that learning should transfer. Although newspapers are not the only reading material which should be approached with this discriminatory set, it is an appropriate set for all newspaper reading. By choosing this answer you have made similar the object in the environment (newspaper), the set to perform (distinguish fact from opinion), and the action of the learner (silent reading of news material) thereby maximizing the possibility of appropriate transfer to future news reading. Turn now to page 34.

d. **You said you would have them identify fact and opinion from statements on a test.**

You are to be congratulated for checking the results of your teaching but how are you providing for transfer to future situations? (Granted if it's not learned it can't transfer.) Think of the future use of the skill and apply what you have learned about similarity promoting transfer. Turn back to the question on page 31 and select an answer that will reflect your knowledge of how to encourage appropriate use of learning in future situations.

Let's summarize what you have read about the possibilities for a learner perceiving a present situation as similar to a past situation and therefore transferring previous learning into current behavior.

Similarity can result from:

A. Factors in the Environmental (objects, people, sounds, time, etc.)

B. Factors within the student (feelings, motivation, set to perform)

C. Factors in the activity of the student (The method of teaching and learning or utilization of a particular sensory mode.)

Simulation is the synthesizing of all of these factors in a situation which approximates as nearly as possible the future situation to which the learning must transfer.

Remember, it is not essential to classify which category is operating because many are involved in every situation. These categories have been identified so you will systematically inspect every possibility for similarity rather than let some unsuspected but potent factor remain undetected.

To give you practice in "detecting" (transfer your set to be alert for all possible clues) here is a list of common behaviors which could be the result of transfer. We use "could be" because nobody knows for sure what is going on in the human brain. Decide which factor of similarity is operating and jot it down. Then identify one thing you could do to make the situation different should you *not* wish transfer to occur. When you have finished, check your answer to see how much your learning from the previous pages has transferred to the following page.

Situation	Factors of Similarity	How to Make Situation Different
	a. environment	
	b. students' feeling or thinking	
	c. students' actions	

1. Although no seats are assigned, students sitting in the same place every day. _____ _____

2. Continuing to write last year's date after January 1. _____ _____

3. Introducing a married friend by her maiden name. _____ _____

4. Calling a new teacher by the former teacher's name. _____ _____

5. People not ordering squid, snails, or frog legs in a restaurant. _____ _____

6. A person, who steers a car well, steering a boat so it leaves a wake that looks like a corkscrew. _____ _____

7. An actor learning lines more rapidly than an equally bright person who has an excellent memory. _____ _____

Turn to page 36 to check your answers.

1. **Although no seats are assigned, students sitting in the same place every day.**

Factor of similarity: environment

Students may have a reason for originally sitting in certain seats (by their friends, so they can see, etc.). Usually from then on it becomes "habit" and their previous behavior transfers to each new class period because the environment is the same.

To change that behavior, rearrange the furniture or take them into a different classroom (although the seats may be arranged the same way). They may choose the same general location but usually will take different seats. If you announce, "Tomorrow you will need to choose different seats," you will be eliciting a different "set to perform" so the old set will not transfer.

2. **Continuing to write last year's date after January 1.**

Factor of similarity: environment and mental set

The same set to perform (date by month, day, year) and the same object in the environment (i.e., the top of the paper or the word "date"), causes the old response to transfer to the new year. We have more trouble with the year than the month because the former has been the only response for a whole year while we have developed the set to change each month. The amount of practice and degree of original learning are also important elements in our error. We will learn more about that shortly.

To eliminate undesirable transfer we must change our set, "Now remember what you need to do differently." We may also write the date in a different place on the paper so the present situation is perceived as requiring a different response. Soon the set to write the new year will transfer to each time we date a paper.

3. **Introducing a married friend by her maiden name.**

Factor of similarity: environment

The same person with the same features and personality triggers the transfer of responding with name originally learned. In the same way, a person after marriage has the problem of giving her maiden name at stores and on the phone. This occurs much less if that person moves or changes jobs immediately after marriage, for the complete change of environment interferes with the routine transfer of old responses.

This response can readily be changed by saying "This is no longer Miss_____ but Mrs._____" which identifies the present as different from the past.

4. Calling a new teacher by the former teacher's name.

Factor of similarity: environment

The objects in the environment, school, pupils, books, desks, remain much the same, so the response of the teacher's name transfers even though it is a different teacher. This seldom happens if the new teacher is of the opposite sex. The differentness becomes more obvious and consequently eliminates transfer caused by similarity. The new teacher can minimize transfer by stressing the ways the present is different from the past.

A substitute teacher developed the strategy of beginning the day by asking the children to tell her about their regular teacher. Then she asks, "Do I look like your teacher?" "Do I talk like your teacher?" To their negatives she responds, "Then I won't do things exactly the same as your teacher." In that way she eliminates all the "that's not the way our teacher does it," static which besieges a substitute.

5. People not ordering squid, snails, or frog legs in a restaurant.

Factor of similarity: feelings

Learning about squid and snails usually is associated with unpleasant adjectives such as "cold, slimy, and gooey." Consequently, those emotionally laden words transfer to the item on the menu and delectable food is rejected. People who have grown up eating those foods associate them with a positive emotional response.

In order to eliminate the negative transfer from past learning, it may be necessary for a person to taste a new food without knowing what it is. Many a person has eaten an Italian dish with gusto only to find out later it was squid. Emotional transfer, however, is very difficult to prevent or change and often people are unable to eliminate transfer of feelings even though they realize those feelings are irrational or incorrect in the current situation.

6. **A person, who steers a car well, steering a boat so it leaves a wake that looks like a corkscrew.**

Factor of similarity: thinking and action

The same general principles related to steering as well as the same mode of attack are transferring to turning the wheel inappropriately. Drivers of cars are used to turning the steering wheel and from the car's immediate response deciding whether or not they need to turn further. The boat's delayed response to steering causes a person to make a premature judgment and turn further only to find out he has "over-done" it. Then he makes the same error as he corrects and continues to turn the wheel too far the other way. The result of such inappropriate transfer is apparent in the wake.

To eliminate this transfer a person has to consciously delay his judgment after turning a boat to see what is going to happen before he turns it further. The same basic principle applies in a boat and a car but the time required for response make direct transfer inappropriate.

7. **An actor learning lines more rapidly than an equally bright person who has an excellent memory.**

Factor of similarity: thinking and action

A successful actor has developed a method of learning his script which he transfers to each new play. The equally bright person has no strategy of learning to call on but must try to assemble skills from his previous memory chores (names, dates, routes, sayings, phone numbers, etc.) and they are not as facilitating to the present task. He will need to develop a strategy for learning lines, then transfer it into future memory tasks for which it is appropriate.

Each occupation, doctor, plumber, attorney, or dressmaker has developed a general strategy for attacking new problems. What works well for one is not usually as effective for another occupation. One of the difficulties in teaching is that only recently have we developed the undergirding strategy which is effective in teaching any learner regardless of age, race, ability, or background. One very important element of this strategy is the use of transfer theory to propel learning. We hope your expertise in this field will continue to develop. This book was written to give that ability an "assist" by describing similar situations and identifying the critical elements of transfer.

38

Now that we have considered the transfer propulsion from similarity of two learning situations, we wish to *change* your focus so we will stress the fact that the next important factor which can influence transfer is related, but it is *different* and is on a different page so turn to page 41.

CHAPTER III

ASSOCIATION OF TWO LEARNINGS

Transfer of Learning is Generated by an Association of Two Learnings.

In the last chapter, we learned about one category of factors which encourages transfer: the perceived similarity of the two learnings. A second category of factors that encourages transfer is an association formed between two learnings even though they may be very different. One learning will tend to transfer to another when for some reason those two learnings are associated by the learner.

For many years, this transfer power has been utilized by advertising. Brand X is used by a handsome man with a fascinating woman. Brand Y is pictured with a man of distinction or demonstrated by just the kind of person the viewer would like to be, strong, verile, rugged or beautiful, slim, sought after. Now, mind you, at no time does the advertising say that if you use brand X or Y you will be that kind of person, the two learnings simply are paired so they will become associated. As a result, millions of dollars worth of products are purchased because the viewer's association of his own desires with brand X and Y transfers to and influences his future buying behavior.

Another example of the transfer power of association is the response that occurs when a situation brings to mind one member of a pair that has been associated in the past. Almost invariably the other member of that pair, even though it may be very different from the first member, transfers to your thoughts or behavior. "Samson" elicits "Delilah," "Snow White" the "Seven Dwarfs."

This phenomenon is so persuasive that "association tests" are used to give clues to the things that have occurred together in an individual's past. Incidently, this book was written to interfere with any "not of any use" associations you may have formed in your past educational psychology classes and to develop in you the new association of psychological theory with "really useful in teaching!"

In daily life we are surrounded by examples of transfer of learning as a result of association. When we see a car coming at us we "put on the brakes" even though we're not driving. New trademarks are made to look the same as successfully established trademarks so the positive "let's buy" feelings associated with the old brand will transfer into purchasing behavior with the new. If a particular motion picture is unusually successful, a similar series is made to elicit the feelings and "movie going" behavior that were associated (learned) with the original film.

Only too vivid is the transfer of feelings and beliefs associated with certain loaded words. Consider the beliefs you automatically transfer to "Bill Jones is a communist," "Ralph Brown is a doctor," "Paul Smith has long hair and plays rock music," "Sara is an artist," "Gene Block is a politician," "That animal is a snake."

Even though you have no knowledge about the person mentioned (he may be a scoundrel or have just jeopardized his life to save another's), you experience the transfer of beliefs and emotions which in the past you have associated with that particular category of person. Prejudice is the transferring of a set of beliefs learned and associated with one category (doctor, politician, snake) to a new situation where they are not necessarily valid or appropriate. On the other hand, this associated learning can positively transfer and be a source of real economy. Knowing that someone is a doctor, you don't have to start from scratch to learn about him but can transfer a great deal of past knowledge associated with doctors into the present situation. Of course, the trick is in knowing which of your associated learnings (i.e. involvement with medical science) are valid for any doctor and which associations are not universal (i.e. area of specialization, appearance, personality).

Whenever associations are formed, knowledge and beliefs may transfer to new situations. If on first encounter one associates a favorable impression with a person, that impression is likely to transfer to future encounters. In the same way, an unpleasant association will transfer and is more difficult to correct if it is erroneous. If Johnny performs well at first, you transfer your opinion of his good behavior into subsequent episodes. If he starts with difficulty you keep a wary eye on him even when he is performing acceptably.

Evidence has established that if a teacher believes a paper was written by an "A" student, it will be graded differently from a paper believed to be from a failing student. Psychologists, in spite of their efforts to be objective, have scored individual intelligence tests lower when they erroneously believed the student was a drop-out than when they believed that same test belonged to a successful learner.

In each case, past associations were transferring to and influencing a present situation. It is extremely important that we constantly monitor what we are "bringing forward" from past learnings and validate that transfer as appropriate and therefore facilitating to the present situation.

Learnings frequently become associated with feelings of joy, fright, sorrow, and excitement. When that same feeling reoccurs a student may perceive the new situation as similar to a past one where he "felt the same way" so the same behavior with which the feeling was originally associated is apt to transfer (appropriately or inappropriately) into the present situation.

The author taught her small son his phone number so that in an emergency he could tell it to any adult and his parents could be reached. Emergency situations in which he would need to give this information were described, such as his becoming lost or separated from his parents, and he practiced responding to questioning by giving an adult his phone number. Subsequently, his first experience with Santa Claus occurred when he was standing in a toy section of a department store. A giant Santa came striding down the aisle and boomed, "Have you been a good boy? What's your name?" This was an emergency if the child had ever seen one so in response he gasped, "GRanite 39715." The feeling of fright had generated transfer of the telephone number even though giving his name was a common and infinitely more practiced response.

Usually the behavior of deliberation and thoughtful action is needed in any situation where emotions are high, yet that behavior seldom occurs at those times. Often, impetuous and thoughtless behavior is associated with stress and, as a result, that behavior transfers into emergencies. Running is associated with fear and negatively transfers into the inappropriate behavior of running from a barking dog. The same inappropriate running behavior results in crowds trampling people in a crisis. To avoid such undesirable transfer, walking and quiet listening behavior are taught in a fire drill so the sound of the alarm and the association of quiet, orderly behavior will transfer to any real fire emergency.

Associations can be formed, as we previously explained, if two learnings occur in the same environment. Another way for learnings to become associated is when they occur at the same time or one right after the other. We may deliberately pair experiences and associate learnings to encourage transfer even though the two learnings seem very different. Recent research in teaching attitudes suggests that if we pair or associate the new learning with something about which an attitude already has been formed, that previous attitude will generalize to the new learning. Consequently, we make an interesting game out of assignments and drills so students' already-learned feeling that "playing games if fun" will transfer into enjoying the math lesson that we teach. We make our classrooms attractive so that the feelings associated with pleasant places will transfer into academic content in the same way that we set a beautiful table to enhance the appetite for food. In opposite fashion the aversive aspect of a dirty environment can be associated with a certain food, transfer, and result in refusal of that same food at a later date. An unhappy or unsuccessful learning experience can be associated, transfer, and result in avoidance of future learning in that subject.

Any association of feelings (pleasure, fear, anxiety, interest) with learning activities can transfer and provide an unexpected accelerent or deterrent to the acquisition of new learning. Consequently, it is important for us always to be alert to the feelings that are being generated in a lesson because those same feelings can by association transfer into other encounters with that subject matter.

At times, association can be deleterious to future learning. For example, being confused and unsure in a certain subject can undesirably transfer to future experiences with that subject even though there is a new teacher who could promote successful learning. All of us can remember unpleasant school experiences which transferred and resulted in "never again!" behavior to that subject. Your college course in statistics is probably an example that is only too vivid!

Feelings and attitudes are especially susceptible to this kind of association and consequent conditioning as they are paired or associated with certain subject areas. These feelings and attitudes tend to generalize and transfer to other experiences in the same or similar subjects. This is one of many reasons why it is important to make school pleasant, interesting, and rewarding, for such feelings become an accelerent to new learning. This is because those feelings generalize from their association with school tasks and transfer into pleasant anticipation or "approach behavior" in other learning situations. Conversely, feelings of frustration and failure in one school situation are apt to generalize or transfer to many other school situations.

"Avoidance behavior" generated by one school subject may transfer to many subjects, or even to the total school program with the resultant "drop-out" from learning.

Teachers who work with remedial students are especially aware of this problem as feelings of previous failure transfer and interfere in a new situation where successful achievement is possible. One of the first remedial objectives to be accomplished is the elimination of this negative transfer so the student will direct his energy to attempting the learning rather than avoiding it. Teachers of students who are beginning a new subject often see eager student effort that is fresh and uncontaminated by a history of problems or past failure associated with the subject. Foreign language teachers experience this phenomenon at the beginning of instruction and can quickly perceive the difference if feelings of difficulty, frustration, and discouragement begin to be associated with the language and transfer to new assignments.

The author experiences this transfer from association for she does most of her writing on airplane flights. Consequently, the association of sitting on a plane triggers writing behavior which always seems much more difficult in her home where social, housekeeping, or family behavior are associated, even though the day has been reserved to "sit down and write." This example could also have been cited with similarity of environment and represents the interaction of several factors.

If we wish to encourage transfer from association of feelings of the past with the present situation, we should make the pairing of the two learnings explicit for the learner. "Remember last week you thought you couldn't figure out the problem but you worked hard and got the right answer? That is what will happen as you work systematically on this problem." By such a verbal pairing of situations, the behavior of putting forth effort and anticipating success is more likely to transfer to the current task.

The statement, "Remember how we got tricked by propaganda last week? Read this carefully!" should elicit the appropriate mental set and transfer skills of critical reading to the present assignment. "Think of your five times tables as buying nickel candy bars," will associate life situations with manipulations of numbers thereby transferring knowledge and associations from those real situations to facilitate the learning of abstract multiplication facts. Creating analogies in terms of the *learner's own life and experience* triggers transfer as he associates and "brings forward" his past understanding to facilitate the present learning.

Verbally specifying the association of one learning with another is one of the most efficient ways of emphasizing that association so that learning from one situation will transfer to the other. "Does working with these maps remind you of something we did last week?" "What did your team do the other time when you didn't have enough players?" "What did the boy in the story do when he was lost? What would you do if you got lost?" All of these statements associate two experiences that may be too dissimilar or distant in time for transfer to occur without teacher prompting. By evoking that association with such verbal pairings, much learning time is saved. Strategies and solutions to one problem can transfer into the resolution of the new situation rather than the learner having to begin from scratch without the assist from previous learnings. We need to emphasize that these focus questions by the teacher are to *stimulate and guide the direction of search*, not to indicate the end product or answer.

Suppose a learner in your group was stuck on a problem that you think he should be able to solve. What would you do?

a. Tell him not to worry, you will give him more time to work on it. ....Turn to page 47, top

b. Tell him to stop and think. ....Turn to page 47, bottom

c. Recall to his mind a previous situation in which he successfully applied the needed skills. ....Turn to page 48, top

d. Help him discover the solution. ......Turn to page 48, bottom

a. You said you would tell him not to worry, you will give him more time to work on it.

It's obvious that he needs time but you may be dealing with eternity (and there are periods in every teacher's life where it seems as if this is the case). You may not have that much time and besides it's an inefficient expenditure of learning energy so turn back to the question on page 46 and select an answer that will speed up his successful performance.

b. You said you would tell him to stop and think.

A thousand teachers before you have done just that. We appreciate your intention to prevent his heedless action but what is he to think about? He may spend his thinking time designing strategies to get out of doing the job altogether. We know you don't want that to happen so turn back to the question on page 46 and select an answer that will encourage him to think about something relevant to the solution of the problem.

c. **You said you would recall to his mind a previous situation in which he successfully applied needed skills.**

Your previous experience in the classroom and/or (we hope!) reading these last few pages has certainly transferred into your action of selecting the correct answer. Focusing the student on a previous situation where he applied the needed skills and associating the important cues in that situation with the current one will encourage the transfer of appropriate learnings. For example, if the learner is stuck on base five in math you might suggest he think about base 10 and the ratio of the 10's to the 1's as well as the ratio of the 100's to the 10's. Having made the ratios in base 10 explicit, the question would follow, "Now how would such relationships apply in base five?" Associating the system of relationships which he already knows with the new problem should assist his ability to deal with the same relationship even though in a different base.

In like manner, recalling to a child's mind a situation when another student forgot his lunch and what the student did about it assists transferring that information into the resolution of an I'm-going-to-die-of-hunger crisis.

Hopefully, calling to your mind typical classroom situations will, by their association with this book, assist transfer of your learning into increasingly expert classroom performance.

For your next "assist" turn to page 49.

d. **You said you would help him discover the solution.**

We're glad he is going to do some discovering and not just be told what to do. Now you need to discover what *you* are going to do to assist him with his discovery process rather than merely hope he is another Columbus. Turn back to the question on page 46 and select the answer that would give him the most productive guidance without telling him exactly what to do.

To assist the student with associating two learnings so one will transfer to the other a teacher must ask two important questions:

1. What has the learner seen, or heard, or felt, or experienced, or done, or learned in the past that would supply positive transfer to this present learning?

2. How could he use that retrieved learning in this new context so the two become associated?

Using examples from a particular learner's own experience (rather than the teacher's experience or the textbook) will recall at a conscious level the similarity of the situations so that those relevant elements of past experience can be identified, transfer, and become associated with the present situation. It is for this purpose that classroom examples rather than laboratory research are cited in this book. (While supporting research is not quoted, it is available to document the generalizations presented.) To associate transfer theory with classroom practice, we need to recall something you have experienced so reality and psychological theory become associated and one will transfer to and propel learning in the other.

For those of you who have ever done knitting or crocheting, we ask you to recall the method of attaching the new row by picking up a stitch from the completed row, so that each new stitch is connected or "hooked into" an old stitch. In the same way, new learnings can be connected to or associated with previous learnings so each will contribute strength to the other.

For those of you who know nothing about crocheting or knitting, this example is not effective because you do not have that past learning to associate with and transfer to the present concept we are presenting. To form an association for you, an example from your own background of experience would be necessary.

One of the major problems in working with children from a poverty culture is that often we do not correctly anticipate the learnings they already have to transfer to our current educational effort. For example, we tell them to do something "on time" assuming that those words will be associated with and trigger previously learned "promptness" behavior. Such students, however, often have no previous learning of "being on time" to associate with the verbal

49

cue so they continue at their own pace or no pace at all. Another source of teacher frustration is the disregard that some children from poverty cultures seem to have for neatness and order. Yet, if we examine their previous learnings, we will see that they come from environments where middle class concepts of order often are nonexistent, and organization in terms of schedules and plans is not possible. Consequently, the poverty child can be as deficient in these learnings as he is in language learning. If in our teaching we anticipate the same "boost" from transfer of past habits that we would get from most middle class children, we are doomed to disappointment.

This does not mean, however, that poverty children cannot learn these new behaviors. It simply means we have to teach each behavior as a new learning rather than expect transfer from past experience. Teachers need to learn about "poverty cultures" not so they are more sympathetic and accepting (although we hope they are) but so they can more correctly anticipate the potential, or lack of it, for positive and negative transfer and plan accordingly for successful learning.

The wise teacher, to propel learning, plans lessons to develop productive associations. It is not always possible to pair learning experiences or connect them in time, yet we wish to teach to provide the riches of such association, not the sterility of simple recall. Here language, man's major cognitive achievement, provides the medium for such association. Verbal pairing, "this is the same as...." or "remember last week when we...." provides a verbal bridge that spans time and space barriers. As we pointed out earlier, labeling the similarity and verbally carrying it into action—"therefore we would ..." or "in these circumstances we could...."—connects cognition with future action. Just because you say you "would" doesn't mean in action you "will," but it's an important step in transfer to future performance.

Let's look at a classroom example of this notion. A teacher wishes students to learn how to use the guide words at the top of the page in a dictionary or telephone directory. He presents two guide words such as "choice" and "church." The student, who has already learned to alphabetize to the third letter, must take a third word such as "charm" and determine whether he would look for it before, after, or in between the two guide words. To maximize transfer of this skill to future "location" endeavors the teacher would:

a. Require the verbal response of "Charm would come before (or after or between)." .... Turn to page 52, top

b. Require that the student verbally identify the letter which gave him the clue to the right response. .... Turn to page 52, bottom

c. Require that the student add, "Therefore I would turn back in the book (or ahead, or find it on this page)." ....
.... Turn to page 53, top

d. Require a page of independent work demonstrating the student's proficiency in the task. .... Turn to page 53, bottom

a. You said to maximize transfer the teacher would require the verbal response of "Charm would come before (or after or in between)."

You certainly have learned that verbalization assists transfer and such a technique is more effective than merely pointing to where the word would occur. The concept of coming before or after needs to be associated with the use of guide words for locating material. You can help a learner associate that concept by having him either say it or demonstrate it in action. There is a better answer, however, because it also incorporates verbalizing what you would do in order to locate the word. Turn back to the question on page 51 and find that answer.

b. You said to maximize transfer the teacher would require that the student verbally identify the letter which gave him the clue to the right response.

By selecting this answer you certainly would eliminate the possibility of focusing on the wrong clue. Focusing on the right clue is an important factor in any discrimination task. We assumed, however, that this skill had already been learned and additional verbalization would only reinforce that learning, not carry it further. Turn back to the question on page 51 and select an answer which will incorporate and associate the future behavior to which this lesson should transfer.

c. **You said to maximize transfer the teacher would require that the student add, "Therefore I would turn back in the book (or ahead, or find it on this page)."**

Right you are! A skill is being learned and "carried by words" into the simulation of action for which that learning was intended. The learner is making a discrimination and then associating it with the directions that will guide him into what to do. This is exactly what will occur (possibly at an automatic, no-longer-verbal level) when later he uses guide words to locate material. If you are wondering why he is involved in two learnings at once (the alphabetizing and verbalizing which way to go in the book), the location of the word in relation to the other two words is the only new learning, and it is being "hooked onto" the already learned skill of turning back or ahead in the book. Transfer is greatly increased by verbalization of the application of the learning to the experience for which it is intended. "Therefore I would" or "under these conditions I will need to" are important stimuli to effective transfer. Of course, later he will need to actually use guide words to find material to be sure the association has been accomplished and transfer has occurred. Your selection of this answer indicates that your knowledge of association has transferred into a real life example, so turn to page 55.

d. **You said to maximize transfer the teacher would require a page of independent work demonstrating the student's proficiency in the task.**

You're wise to validate learning rather than just make an assumption that it has occurred. You would know that the students could place the word correctly, but will this transfer to the times they need this skill for locating material? If you're like most teachers you will respond, "I certainly hope so!" "Hope" is no longer enough; we must design a lesson that incorporates high probability for that transfer. Turn back to the question on page 51 and select an answer where you don't have to "hope" but can "see to it" that the student is associating the behavior he will need in every future situation where he is using guide words to locate material.

CHAPTER IV

DEGREE OF ORIGINAL LEARNING

We have considered two factors which stimulate transfer of learning: the similarity of situations and the association of two learnings. A third important factor in transfer is the degree of original learning, *for the degree of transfer is related to the degree of effectiveness of the original learning.*

Unfortunately, much of what is "taught" is only half-learned and consequently does not transfer correctly or effectively to a new situation where that learning is appropriate. A classic example is the young child who is learning about "kitty" transferring that learning to a skunk. Not so obvious but equally lethal to learning are the many "covered" but not-learned lessons which do not transfer when they should, or transfer inappropriately and interfere with new learning. Examples of this confusion are students who "carry" or "borrow" in a problem where no regrouping is necessary, those who "spray" commas throughout a composition, and those who engage in complex and intricate activities when the solution is a simple one. The better something is learned, the more that learning is apt to transfer *appropriately* into future learnings. Poorly learned material if it transfers at all, is more likely to transfer *in*appropriately and result in interference with new learning. (One person's name transfers to another person's face when you have met many people at a meeting and have not had time enough to sort them out, but your best friend's name does not transfer to another person with a similar appearance.) The obvious inference from this transfer factor of degree of original learning is that anything we are going to teach should be taught so it is well learned, not "once over lightly." The virtuous feeling of "at least exposing them to it" can become the vice of "confusing them by it" as incomplete learnings negatively transfer and interfere with other learning. ("Now let's see, which one do you turn upside down when you invert the division and multiply?")

Adequate learning usually is not accomplished in one exposure so we may need to return to a concept many times and see it in many differing situations before it is well enough understood to transfer to other situations where it is appropriate. The more completely we learn one task, the more likely that mastery is to transfer and facilitate learning another task. As a result, the time it takes to learn the second task is substantially decreased. In this book we will not focus on the principles a teacher can employ to ensure an adequate degree of learning as those principles are developed in detail in *Teach More— Faster!* of this series.

Well learned material usually is complete, accurate, meaningful, and structured, consequently is less susceptible to negative transfer. Therefore, we should complete one learning to an appropriate degree before introducing another related learning. If something important is not well learned we would be wiser to spend more time on it and delay or, if necessary, skip the next learning. Research indicates that time devoted to successful learning on an easier task will yield better transfer to the accomplishment of a related difficult task than the same amount of time spent only on the difficult task. This is an important reason why learners should never be "in over their heads" and struggling with a learning task that is too difficult.

Learning something well is especially important if two learnings are to be differentiated (not confused with each other). A student should accomplish one learning before going on to another (knowing "went" before trying to learn "want"). A bright child usually learns faster, therefore his learning tends to be more complete so he transfers and differentiates more easily. A less able learner does not learn as fast, therefore his learning may not be complete. As a result of incomplete learning (not necessarily his native ability) he cannot differentiate situations, and past learning transfers inappropriately or not at all.

To cite a previous example, if we are introduced to one woman and then to her twin sister we experience difficulty in telling them apart. We transfer the name of one to the other and often when we think we are talking to one we find we are in conversation with the other. The twins' husbands have none of this difficulty. Each knows immediately if it is his wife or her sister. Knowledge of his own wife is so effectively learned there is no negative transfer or confusion with her sister. This may not have been true when they first met their wives.

Let's look at an example of this phenomenon in a school situation. A group of Inner City children were enrolled in the University Nursery School and were introduced for the first time to a pet duck. They were delighted with this feathered novelty as they plunked him in a tub of water and saw him bob about despite friendly attempts to sink him. A short time later the teacher needed to rescue a water-logged rooster who was receiving the same treatment. The children's new learning with one feathered pet had inappropriately transferred to another. As they gained experience with both pets they had no

56

difficulty behaving appropriately with each. A subsequent visit to a farm revealed completed learning as ducks were put in the pond, roosters were left on land but grain was fed to both.

Now let's look at an example of how incomplete learning may have transferred to and affected your own teaching behavior. Knowledge of evaluation techniques for different purposes usually is inadequately learned in college. Consequently, we find that learning does not transfer appropriately or efficiently to daily classroom evaluation. A complex and costly testing program may be necessary for district survey purposes but is not necessary to answer daily instructional questions. "What should I teach?" is determined by what each student already knows and where he should direct his present learning energy. Because teachers have not developed an adequate understanding of diagnostic teaching, we find knowledge about standardized achievement tests transferring inappropriately to daily classroom instructional decisions. ("I can't group my class until the achievement tests have been given.")

An equally vivid instance of inefficient transfer from the degree of teachers' original learning is the partially learned generalizations that result from most courses in educational psychology or learning theory. Because it is not well understood, psychological theory is almost useless to most teachers in solving learning problems in the classroom. In fact, that college psychology course may have been taught in a way that violated all the principles in this book.

If evaluation techniques and psychological principles are well learned, each will transfer more successfully and effectively into daily teaching behavior. Again, we need to stress that the categories of similarity, association, and degree of learning which encourage transfer are not mutually exclusive. The similarity of the college lecture course and association with the problems encountered in a real classroom leave much to be desired.

The recent push to get future teachers into a classroom earlier in their training is an effort to solve the problem of similarity of the environment in which something is learned and the environment to which that learning should transfer. This similarity of environment, however, will not necessarily solve the factor of the degree of effectiveness of original learning. Consequently, earlier or more frequent classroom experience does not guarantee valid and successful application of psychological theory in practice. It may, in fact, produce the opposite result as teaching errors become associated with classroom problems. Following the principles in this book, theory must be taught in such a manner that those factors which promote transfer will be utilized in teacher education classes so resultant learning will yield positive transfer for future teaching behavior.

Now let's apply this notion of achieving an adequate degree of learning to an important objective of contemporary education; that the learner become increasingly responsible for and in charge of his own educational growth. This objective is not accomplished by wishful thinking nor is it a result of simply providing an environment where it can happen. As with all learning, independence in learning is the result of a cluster of escalating competencies which are learned in increments. To become an independent learner, the student must (1) identify the alternatives from which he can choose, (2) select one, (3) gather the necessary learning materials, (4) select an appropriate space to work, (5) sustain focus on the task, (6) complete it to *his* satisfaction, and (7) put materials away when finished. If the learner has not achieved the first skill of selecting a task or gathering needed materials, little progress toward independence is likely to be achieved.

Assuming that you have a class with the typical range of skills in this area (from zero to a few independent learners) how would you go about teaching these skills so they would transfer into each new activity?

a. Begin with only two or three choices then increase the number of possibilities for those students who demonstrate skill in productive independence. ....Turn to page 59, top

b. Begin with two or three choices verbally labeling each step or procedure. Then as students engage in independent activity, encourage them to make explicit (i.e., "I'm going to work on _____ and I'll need_____"). As some students gain proficiency, introduce those students to additional possibilities having them practice and label the series of decisions and actions in which they are engaged.... Turn to page 59, bottom

c. Provide a wide variety of choices so students will have a chance to generalize their skill of independent learning to many different situations. ....Turn to page 60, top

d. Have students practice making a choice and assembling materials in many different situations. After they had learned those skills, teach them to focus on the task and accomplish something to their satisfaction. ....Turn to page 60, bottom

a. **You said you would begin with only two or three choices then increase the number of possibilities for those students who demonstrate skill in productive independence.**

You are wise to limit the possibilities of choice until some competence is demonstrated. This is a correct application of the concept that the greater the degree of original learning the greater the appropriate transfer. But what are you going to do to insure that the essential skills are identified so they will more efficiently transfed to new activities? Unfortunately just being exposed to the possibility does not always enhance the probability of learning. Some students will remain at their original level of incompetence unless you do something to help them. Turn back to the question on page 58 and select an answer where you apply what you have learned about factors which increase the probability of transfer.

b. **You said you would begin with two or three choices verbally labeling each step of the procedure. Then as students engage in independent activity, you would encourage them to make explicit ("I'm going to work on_____ _____and I'll need_____ ").
As students gain proficiency, you would introduce those students to additional possibilities having them practice and label the series of decisions and actions in which they are engaged.**

A great deal of previous learning has transferred into your selection of this answer (1) making situations similar, (2) associating two learnings and labeling that association, and (3) achieving an adequate degree of learning before moving on. You made situations similar by teaching activities with labels and then having students engage in those activities supplying the same labels. (Obviously, this labeling reflects thoughtful decision making not chanting a recitation.) You associated good work habits (labeled) with independent activities (which often are not associated with productive work habits). As students demonstrated an adequate degree of learning, you gave them opportunities to transfer that behavior to new situations.

If you put into action the principles of this answer, we guarantee you'll see a growth of productive independence in your classroom that will amaze you. Turn now to page 61 to learn about the fourth, and by far the most important, factor that generates transfer.

c. **You said you would provide a wide variety of choices so students will have a chance to generalize their skills of independent learning to many different situations.**

You are correct in assuming that students must have the opportunity to generalize or transfer their skills but you have the cart before the horse. First, they must have the opportunity to learn those skills. Otherwise you may find they are transferring all kinds of nonproductive behavior such as not sticking with a job long enough to accomplish anything or starting heedlessly with insufficient space or materials. Turn back to the question on page 58 and select the answer that indicates what you would do first.

d. **You said you would have students practice making a choice and assembling materials in many different situations. After they had learned those skills you would teach them to focus on the task and accomplish something to their satisfaction.**

You certainly have the notion of accomplishing one thing before beginning the next, but in this case it's working and achieving satisfaction that makes choices and materials meaningful. If you will recall what you learned about practice in *Teach More—Faster!* of this series, you'll realize that you practice as much of a task as will establish maximum meaning. Chopping a task into meaningless or purposeless units makes it more difficult to learn.

The reason we included this answer was that we were aware that the generalization, "make sure each step is well learned before you move on" could transfer inappropriately and result in chopping up a meaningful task into meaningless components.

Turn back to the question on page 58 and select an answer where each part is well learned but the integrity of making choices and accomplishing something is maintained.

CHAPTER V

IDENTIFICATION OF ESSENTIAL AND
UNVARYING ELEMENTS

We have learned about three factors that promote transfer: (1) the similarity of situations, (2) the association of learnings, and (3) the degree of original learning.

A fourth factor which promotes transfer is the presence of critical, essential and unvarying elements in two learnings. *Transfer is generated by the identification of essential and unvarying elements which signal that a past learning has relevance and is applicable to a present situation.* We have all experienced such sensations as "I haven't seen him for years but I'd know his walk anywhere", "I didn't recognize her until I heard her voice", and "The minute I saw the painting I knew it was a Picasso." In each case, although the new situation was very different, some invariant quality signaled that our previous knowledge was applicable because the unfamiliar situation was (in spite of its differentness) similar to a situation that had been learned in the past. Sometimes these critical qualities are explicit and perceivable such as a "walk" or a "voice." Sometimes the quality is not so explicit but it is still perceivable as in a painting.

The critical or invariant element may be a specific property such as the tail design of a particular aircraft which insures recognition of that aircraft regardless of the variance of other conditions. The invariant element also can be a generalization such as "fish breathe through gills" which transfers to the identification of a whale as *not* a fish regardless of its fishlike appearance or living in the ocean. The identification of the essential or unvarying element on which the learner should focus, or the particular cues which provide the basis for discrimination in order to deal appropriately with the situation, yields real economy and efficiency in learning. Because it is so important, this process of identification of critical elements must not be left to chance. Focusing on associated but nonessential or extraneous elements accounts for much negative transfer with resultant confusion and inefficiency in learning.

An example of this negative transfer which results from not focusing on the critical discriminatory element is the common student error of writing "there books" and "they went their" or "its" for "it's." This happens because usually sound *is* the critical element in correct spelling. In words such as these, however, it is not sound but meaning which supplies the essential cue on which the learner must focus to correctly transfer his past learning to the present situation.

A popular version of this ability to focus on the essential element which acts as the critical discriminator is the story of the old lady who exclaimed about the baby in the park "I know it's a boy because his blanket is blue!" To which a bystander responded, "Madam, science has identified a more infallible discriminator." We, too, experience this confusion for we used to operate successfully from the discriminator, "Girls have longer hair and boys wear pants." Now this generalization is no longer useful.

The purpose of identifying the critical elements or generalization in a situation, idea, thing, or whatever we encounter is to reduce the complexity of the world around us so we can appropriately transfer our past learning to deal productively and economically with the present rather than having to begin anew with each experience.

Developing valid generalizations increases the efficiency of learning because generalizations promote appropriate transfer and eliminate the distractive impact of nonessential detail which can vary in each situation. Generalizations are verbal road signs that lead a student's focus to the essential elements which make each situation what it is. (Example: A topic sentence tells you what the paragraph is about.) In contrast, teaching which emphasizes particular items or generalizations which may be common but are not essential is educationally barren teaching and produces little productive transfer. (Example: A topic sentence is often the first sentence in the paragraph. This generalization, while it is correct, focuses a student on the wrong property. As a result, he can err in identifying the topic sentence.)

If the teacher is aware that generalizations occur, and not all possible generalizations are equally useful, then control and direction should be maintained as we teach for positive transfer.

In a very simple form, these examples indicate the essence of transfer power which can be derived from the identification of critical elements or generalizations that *make a situation what it is* and thereby enable a learner to apply his knowledge to new situations where it is appropriate and avoid the pitfall of erroneous application (i.e., a kitten for a skunk, a gopher snake for a rattler, the first sentence for the topic sentence, or a comma for a semicolon).

Such transfer of learning is essential for no school can anticipate, much less provide for, every future life situation which the learner will encounter.

The identification of essential and unvarying elements is probably the most important concept in this book. *The reason is that identification of a critical element or invariance is a factor which can be deliberately incorporated in a teaching situation so its accomplishment can be brought under instructional control,* while the factors of perception of *similarities, associations,* and *degree of learning* are not so subject to instructional control.

Though we teach for *identification of similarities,* we cannot control everything the learner perceives as similar. For example, after telling the story of Little Red Riding Hood, the teacher asked a group of five-year-olds what their mother did that was like Red Riding Hood's mother. The teacher was seeking responses such as "She tells us to go straight to school," or "not to talk to strangers," or "to go a certain way and not to stop to do other things." One five-year-old boy responded, "Because she bought me a sweater." The teacher was wise enough to ask, "How was that the same?" and the response came, "The sweater was red."

In like manner, regardless of the teacher's intent, unwanted *associations* sometimes can be formed. At recess a team loses an important ball game. Immediately afterwards the unknowing teacher introduces some new content. The players' feelings of anger and humiliation are associated with their first exposure to that new content so in the future, an encounter with that content could trigger those associations of anger and unpleasantness. Such unplanned for associations are only too common. We are introduced to a new food in unpleasant surroundings and become conditioned to avoid the food in the future.

A kindergarten teacher experienced this unforeseen association when a cooperative child refused, with cement stubbornness, to walk or balance on a 2 x 4 board. Later investigation revealed that at home he had attempted to walk on the top rail of his fence. He had fallen, hurt himself, been humiliated and scolded by his mother. The similarity of the 2 x 4 with the unpleasant associations had transferred and resulted in his rejection of an easy task. Such associations often are in back of unpredictable or unexplainable behavior at school.

As we consider the third factor promoting transfer, the *degree of original learning,* we are increasingly, through our application of basic principles of learning, able to influence the rate and degree of a student's learning. Still, learning is not yet as predictable as we would desire. As teachers, we *do control,* however, our attention to, selection, and implementation of learning experiences that are focused on identification of *essential and unvarying elements,* rather than extraneous detail. We cannot guarantee that every student will learn those unvarying elements but we can guarantee that more will learn them with resultant positive transfer if we teach for identification of those elements, than if we just hope they will be discovered. Teaching so generalizations and key elements will more predictably be discovered should be a major educational goal.

How *do* we teach to identify the invariants which signal that a past learning is appropriate to a present situation? How do we achieve the learning economy that occurs when a student doesn't have to start each learning anew, but can apply knowledge learned in one situation to many other situations where that same learning is appropriate? How do we insure that the learner recognize in the new situation certain key elements which signal that it is the same as some previously learned situation even though most of the elements in the new situation may be different from the student's previous experience?

To discharge our responsibility for enabling the learner to identify, make explicit, and verbally label those critical cues which signal that a previous learning is appropriate and will facilitate learning in a new situation, we must teach our students:

1. to categorize: group by certain properties,
2. to identify critical properties or invariants which make some-thing what it is,
3. to deal with more complex situations as a result of predifferen-tiation training in simpler situations,
4. to operate from those generalizations which are relevant to the critical attributes of a situation,
5. to make explicit and label the attributes which are guiding him in each of the above four skills.

64

While many of these skills interact in a learning situation, we'll look at each separately so see how we might incorporate such objectives in our daily teaching.

1. Categorization

One of man's most important thinking skills is his ability to categorize. The ability to group objects or ideas according to properties or qualities enables us to simplify the complexity in our environment and, when appropriate, deal with perceivably different things as if they were the same. Such categories as nations, mammals, principles of learning, and strategies for teaching enable us to transfer a great deal of learning from one situation into another situation which belongs to the same category in spite of the many differences in particular members or situations within that category.

We may begin teaching categorization by having students sort objects into piles by color, shape, size, texture, or any other property. The use of objects with perceivable properties is a beginning step for the more complex process of grouping when properties are not so tangible or obvious. Learners need practice in identifying the invariant property or similarity which determines whether or not something belongs to a particular group or category. Once that property or characteristic is established it simplifies dealing with our environment because we can ignore much of the complexity and not be distracted by it. For example, once we establish that we are categorizing by color, even a three-year-old can transfer his skill to grouping new objects ignoring the variables of size, shape, weight, texture, etc.

Learners of any age can develop the ability to categorize and thereby maximize transfer potential. As the learner matures, he should be able to deal with increasingly complex and abstract properties of objects or situations. Unfortunately, many adults have not had the opportunity to develop the skill of simplifying complexity by dealing with ideas and objects in categories or groups identified by an invariant characteristic. We find many educators confusing the category of what-you're-trying-to-accomplish with how-you're-going-to-do-it. As a result, we engage in hot arguments about "telling vs. discovering," "lectures vs. discussion," "independent vs. group activity," which all belong to the "how" category. There is no point in even considering the category of "how" until you have dealt with the "what" category in terms of the learning to be accomplished. Much of our educational conflict and disagreement results from inability to categorize our questions and thereby recognize on which part of the problem we are focused. In short, we have not learned well enough the discriminators which identify different aspects of teaching or the generalizations that affect those aspects. Consequently, negative transfer occurs and we confuse problems of *what* we are trying to teach with solutions appropriate to *how* we teach. As a result, inappropriate knowledge from past experience transfers and we unintentionally commit educational errors or make nonproductive decisions.

Another problem which has been identified as an interference to thinking and learning has been the one aptly described as "hardening of the categories." This refers to a person's inability to shift from a more common or highly visible property or quality to a less obvious one when the latter is the critical basis for the correct response. Students need to learn that there are many possibilities and there exists no single correct way to categorize or group objects or situations. It depends on the critical element which is in focus. If learners sort objects by color, they need to be able to re-sort them by size, then by weight, then by texture, etc. By doing this they are more likely to develop the intellectual flexibility so necessary for creative solutions to problems, for an important element in the solution of any problem is the ability to deal with it in a systematic and orderly way but one that is not rigid or constricted. Learning which is focused on the processes of analyzing, categorizing and generalizing yields tremendous transfer potential to future learning efficiency.

Reinforcing a learner for choosing a relevant but not typically preferred or seldom used basis for solving a problem helps him to choose that basis later when again it is relevant to solving the problem. Always using the same basis or orientation may result in a rigid or restricted approach to problem solving and actually interfere with consideration of alternatives and selection of the one most appropriate for the current situation.

Let's practice developing some skills of categorizing. Incidentally, this type of practice is excellent intellectual exercise for any age learner. Use it in those odds and ends of time just before lunch or at the end of a rainy, windy day when a provocative game is the only activity that will keep the group focused and attending.

Which three of the following objects belong in the same category and why would the critical attribute of that category exclude the fourth object?

table

door

chair

refrigerator

a. table, door, chair ....Turn to page 68

b. door, chair, refrigerator ....Turn to page 68

c. table, door, refrigerator ....Turn to page 68

d. table, chair, refrigerator ....Turn to page 68

If you had a difficult time deciding which three went together, it could be for two reasons: (1) You may have such flexibility of thinking that you could group any three in a category which would exclude the fourth. If so, you are facile in categorization and should experience many benefits to your thinking and learning, or (2) you may have been experiencing negative transfer from your previous knowledge that all four are commonly found in a house. As a result, you had difficulty in focusing on less prominent or common properties which would have enabled you to group three of them and exclude the fourth.

There are many possibilities; we will list only a few.

a. Table, door, and chair belong to the category of articles where wood is the most common construction material *or* whose temperature is the same as the room around them *or* in most cases they are easily moved. Each of these attributes excludes refrigerators.

b. Door, chair, and refrigerator belong to the category of articles where one's first visual impression is usually vertical rather than horizontal *or* their names do not have the letter "b" but do have "r" *or* they (or parts of them) often move in use. Each of these attributes excludes tables.

c. Table, door, and refrigerator belong to the category of articles which usually present a smooth flat visual impresssion *or* whose names have no consonant diagraphs (ch) *or* where openings to, or storage surfaces, or both are incorporated in the object. Each of these attributes excludes chairs.

d. Table, chair, and refrigerator belong to the category of articles whose horizontal surfaces provide their main utility *or* which usually have contact points with the floor *or* are associated with eating. Each of these attributes excludes doors.

No doubt you have thought of other ways to categorize these objects. Obviously, there is no one way which is right until you determine your purpose. Our purpose was to have you experience the thinking skill which is basic to discovering and using critical or invariant properties as a way of grouping to simplify complexity. Once you have identified and made explicit the critical attribute of the category you could deal with everything else in a house on the basis of the grouping.

Try this "intellectual exercise" in your classroom. At first, work with objects whose categories you have thought through in advance. Even then you'll be surprised by new categories generated by your students. Later you can ask four students to each contribute the name of one object in the classroom or from the world at large. The class can practice developing categories using three objects and excluding one. You'll be amazed at the "educational yield" from their (and your) attempts to categorize. As students gain proficiency, you can work with famous people, events, even theories and ideas.

2. Identification of Critical Attribute

In order to make sure a learner is appropriately transferring previous knowledge rather than just a vague feeling about a present situation, he should identify and label the critical attribute which makes that situation "what it is."

An example of such explicitness was the training given to aircraft spotters in World War II. These people needed to recognize planes from all angles and in any situation. Such discriminations, presented a tremendous learning feat until the critical property of each aircraft was made explicit and taught to the spotters. Then, regardless of the tremendous variance in situations or modifications of appearance in aircraft, recognition and identification became a relatively simple process. Learning had been accomplished in such a way that it transferred appropriately into each new and never before encountered situation.

The profession of education is an outstanding example of lack of this thinking skill of identifying critical attributes, for often we are attracted to or distracted by each new gimmick or organizational plan and fail to look for the critical educational attribute of "will it increase learning?" As a result, many educational innovations are incorporated in a program when they are not well understood and instead of producing increased learning, produce negative transfer, interfere with previous good practice and result in educational chaos. (Does it sound familiar?)

Because of the transfer propulsion from key elements or generalizations, and the resultant economy in learning, we should seek such elements and generalizations whenever they exist. We need to make sure that learners focus on and label essential cues rather than non-essential ones so those critical attributes may be used to deal with future situations where they are applicable. We cannot overemphasize the mediating power of language in labeling such discriminators. "A crocodile has a pointed snout; an alligator's is rounded," will give the learner the power to discriminate between any alligator and crocodile regardless of other distracting conditions.

It is essential that the learner really perceive the essential features (rather than "parroting" them) and isolate those discriminators from the sometimes dramatic and vivid but incidental and irrelevant features of specific cases. To accomplish this learning, a single illustration is seldom sufficient but many examples need to be presented which require the learner to identify the critical element and make the discrimination. Then the learner should practice these discriminations in ways which are as similar as possible to the ways he will be using them in the future.

Let's look at some examples of teaching where the learner identifies and responds to the transfer power of essential elements and invariant properties.

A learner's knowledge of base ten should transfer into his regrouping (or carrying) behavior. In the operation of addition, the significant cue is whether the sum of any column is more than nine. If learners were focused on this property, they would check each column for that attribute rather than indiscriminately carrying for every problem on the page regardless of whether such behavior is appropriate. We should also include in each assignment problems where sums are less than nine so the learner is not routinely (and unthinkingly) applying his new skill to a page of "problems where you carry." Unfortunately in too much practice, the learner doesn't have to apply the critical generalization or discrimination, but simply proceeds by recipe and does the same thing to each example.

After teaching this attribute, which signals that the learner must "carry," we need to test his degree of learning with an assignment that includes problems where the sum in no column is over nine, problems where the sum is more than nine only in the ones column, problems where the sum is more than nine only in the tens column, problems where every column has a sum of more than nine, etc. Focus on this significant discriminator should eliminate indiscriminate regrouping as well as correcting for the learner who can "carry" in the ones column but is not able to transfer that same skill to the hundreds column.

Let's test your skill in identifying a critical attribute or essential discriminator. All of us are familiar with the inexperienced or remedial reader's confusion between "was" and "saw." Our previous learning in this book explains such negative transfer. The objects (letters) are the same and are first experienced together in the same kind of simple sentences (Bill—a dog) so the two words are associated. Both words usually are introduced in a preprimer so often an adequate degree of learning has not been achieved.

Regardless of whether you have ever taught reading, you should be able to answer our question. If you wanted to eliminate a learner's confusion between "was" and "saw" would you:

a. Have him focus on the letters? . . . . Turn to page 72, top
b. Have him focus on the meaning of the sentence? . . . .
. . . . Turn to page 72, bottom
c. Have him look more closely? . . . . Turn to page 73, top
d. Have him look at the first letter? . . . . . . Turn to page 73, bottom

a. You said you would have him focus on the letters.

The letters are certainly essential elements in words but in this case the actual letters are identical. The "a" occurs in the middle with a "w" on one side and an "s" on the other. In fact, his focusing on *just* the letters is what is negatively transferring and making him unable to tell one word from the other. Turn back to the question on page 71 and select the answer that will focus him on the element which will make it impossible to call one word the other.

b. You said you would have him focus on the meaning of the sentence.

Focusing on meaning is probably the most important factor in developing word attack skills and one which is often neglected. In the case of "was" and "saw," however, it may not help. Using meaning as the key discriminator you could figure out "Bill—a piano" but not "Bill—a dog." Unfortunately, meaning often will not discriminate between "was" and "saw" so turn back to the question on page 71 and select an answer that will provide an infallible clue.

c. You said you would have him look more closely.

You are certainly right, the essential clue is a visible one but what is he to look at? He may frantically look at the picture, the next sentence, or your face, all of which may be of some help but certainly cannot be depended upon to supply the correct word. Go back to the question on page 71 and select an answer which will give the specific information of what he is to look at.

d. You said you would have him look at the first letter.

Your knowledge of critical attributes has positively transferred to your selection of this answer. The critical discriminator between "was" and "saw" is the order of the letters from left to right. Actually just the first letter provides an infallible discriminator. Once a student learns to focus on this critical attribute he can eliminate the error. The more he practices using this discriminator, the more predictably correct will be his differentiation.

Needless to say, getting meaning from the written word (rather than being able to make the correct series of sounds), is the paramount objective in reading. We assume this has already been accomplished so we might give additional differentiation training by writing a "w" and asking which word it was going to be. Focusing on a simpler part of a more complex whole is known as *pre-differentiation training* and contributes importantly to transfer.

Turn to page 74 to learn how you can incorporate predifferentiation training in your teaching.

3. Predifferentiation Training

At times it is effective to plan "predifferentiation" training, i.e., preliminary practice in distinguishing between the critical elements of a complex task, accompanied by the verbal labeling of those elements before engaging in the total task. This is what we are doing when we ask a child to differentiate "w—" and "s—" without the complexity of the rest of the word.

Predifferentiation training is especially important when the task to be learned is a complex one. Practice on simpler tasks involving the critical discriminations will produce more gain on a complex task than will be produced by a same amount of practice on only the complex task. Needless to say, the motivation of the learner will be increased as he achieves success on the simpler task rather than experiencing discouragement as he attempts to tackle the complex one with no predifferentiation training.

Again, indicating the interaction of factors promoting transfer, we could refer you back to our example of solving word problems in arithmetic. It is effective and efficient to give learners predifferentiation training on each element in the solution of a problem: (a) the question asked, (b) the relevant facts, and (c) the operation to perform with those facts before the more complex task of "solve the word problems on page_____" is assigned.

Working with simple diagrams or photographs before attempting to identify a plane in flight would be another example of predifferentiation training. As you read, you will think of countless examples in your own classroom only you probably didn't know the label "predifferentiation training." Learning that label as well as why it is effective will increase your conscious transfer of such learning propulsion to each new lesson you plan.

In teacher education, we take advantage of the transfer propulsion from predifferentiation training. For example, we train student teachers to distinguish between a question eliciting simple recall (Who was Magellan?) and one that requires higher cognitive processes (In what way was Magellan similar to Daniel Boone?). Such predifferentiation training will produce more transfer to appropriate questioning techniques in the classroom than would be produced by introducing skillful questioning for the first time in the complexity of the teaching act. To insure maximum transfer, the contribution of differing levels of questioning to good teaching should be well learned by the student teacher while the predifferentiation training in types of questions is progressing.

74

This book has attempted to put into practice this recently discovered generalization related to predifferentiation training. You, as a reader, have been focused on the elements that promote transfer and have had them identified in very simple examples. Hopefully, you have learned to recognize them and label them without the complexity or the distractions of a classroom. After you have learned the generalization about one element that promotes transfer, you have been asked questions to test the *degree* of your learning. Only after you know these generalizations and can detect the presence of an element with transfer potential would we expect you to see the *similarity* to your classroom situations so this knowledge will transfer to your daily teaching performance. We have paired the theory with classroom examples so *association* will assist that transfer. Only with application in your own planning and performance, however, will you become skilled in focusing on *critical elements* promoting transfer and using *invariant properties* of classroom situations to increase the economy and effectiveness of your teaching regardless of the variance of subject, age, or type of learner, to say nothing of all the other distractors in a school situation.

Let's develop some *associations* with the application of predifferentiation training right now.

Suppose you were teaching students to read numbers to the millions. While they can read three place numbers well, they get all mixed up if the numerals are in the thousands or millions place. Errors such as reading 1,000,000 for 100,000 or 110,000 for 1,100 often occur. If you were going to do some predifferentiation training with students who could comfortably read 110 and 101 would you:

a. Give them a great deal of practice with all kinds of numbers?
. . . . Turn to page 76, top

b. Have them read the thousands with no mistakes before you presented numbers in the millions?. . . . Turn to page 76, bottom

c. Have them work with groups of dashes instead of numerals indicating whether the dashes between commas would be read as hundreds, thousands, or millions?. . . . . . Turn to page 77, top

d. Have them practice differentiating between 110 and 101, 98 and 980? . . . . Turn to page 77, bottom

a. You said you would give them a great deal of practice with all kinds of numbers.

After the students have learned the discriminator which differentiates the hundreds, thousands, and millions, they will need to practice so their skills are well learned. If they practice before they can tell the difference, they will be practicing errors. One of the most important decisions about practice is whether or not students have learned enough to practice correctly. In this case they obviously haven't so turn back to the question on page 75 and select an answer that will teach them the critical discriminator they will use to differentiate hundreds from millions.

b. You said you would have them read the thousands with no mistakes before you presented numbers in the millions.

You are experiencing negative transfer from the generalization about degree of original learning, and erroneously applying the notion that you must teach one thing well before you move on to the next. In this case the learning you are trying to achieve is the differentiation of thousands and millions. If students read only numbers in the thousands, they will not have to differentiate them from millions and consequently will not be doing the thing you wish them to learn. Your idea of starting with an easier task is correct, however. Turn back to the question on page 75 and select an answer which has them practice the critical discrimination in a simple form.

c. You said you would have them work with groups of dashes instead of numerals, indicating whether the dashes between commas would be read as hundreds, thousands, or millions.

We guarantee that by such a procedure, your students will learn that position is the key discriminator which tells the value of a number. Using a series of dashes (---, ---, ---,) pointing to one group and having the students verbalize "thousands" or "millions" is excellent predifferentiation training that excludes the distractor of the complexity of reading the numerals.

Next you would take a three place number such as 114 and place it in varying positions between commas so students could practice using the position discriminator while reading numbers. Finally you would advance to the complexity of reading different numerals in each position. Not until that was mastered would you add those confounding (and confounded) zeros sprinkled through.

Your choice of this answer should transfer into all your teaching and constantly trigger the question, "How can I teach for predifferentiation so students focus on and practice using the critical element that must transfer to differentiate more complex situations?"

Turn to page 78 for some predifferentiation training in the critical generalizations about teaching generalizations.

d. You said you would have them practice differentiating between 110 and 101, 98 and 980.

If they did not have this skill, it would be the appropriate place to begin. Our question indicated, however, that they could read three place numbers well and it was the position of the numerals in relation to commas that was giving them trouble. Turn back to the question on page 76 and select an answer that will reflect transfer of your knowledge of predifferentiation training to this situation.

4. Generalizations

We are constantly admonished to "teach for generalizations." The reason is that a generalization is transferable to many situations. Look at the difference between statements such as "Whenever Bill makes a smart remark, the kids laugh so he keeps on doing it" and "Whenever attention getting behavior is successful, it will increase." While both statements are valid generalizations, the second statement is useful in any situation where a student is making a bid for attention (smart remarks, whining, clowning, clothes, appearance, etc.) so the teacher can transfer previous learning about reinforcement theory to improve any behavior rather than having each problem present a different teaching puzzle.

An example of a powerful generalization in teaching is, "Check what a learner already knows to determine what he should learn next." This generalization will enable a teacher to ignore such popular and overworked distractors as age, grade level, and I.Q. which often can suggest inappropriate learning tasks. The competent teacher may intuitively be following this valid diagnostic procedure but "putting it in words" as a generalization increases the probability that it will transfer to every teaching situation. (Currently many teachers follow this generalization in reading but may ignore it in math or spelling.)

A caution should be stated here; mere parroting of the words of a generalization does not mean it is understood and will transfer to new situations. Remember something must be well learned to transfer appropriately. Applying a generalization in different situations, discriminating between several pictures of crocodiles and alligators, or assessing student achievement in many situations then using that information to plan the next learning opportunity for those students insures focus on and understanding of key discriminators as well as develops the ability to ignore distractors, no matter how tempting. ("Yes, but he should be in the 6th grade book.")

Some generalizations are concerned with common or unvarying elements and give us information about a category which can be transferred to any member of that category. Cars have four wheels. People need food to eat and air to breathe. Wool makes warm clothing. Such generalizations can be transferred to any car, person, or wool garment. They do not, however, differentiate cars from wagons, people from animals, or wool garments from other warm clothing. Nevertheless, such generalizations are useful because they provide valid information which can be transferred to anything that belongs to the category.

Another kind of generalization is one which is true only for members of a category and therefore differentiates that category from any other. This kind of generalization is concerned with the critical attributes of a category which "make it what it is." A car is designed primarily for transportation of small groups of people. Only people (not animals) store and retrieve knowledge. Wool comes from sheep. These generalizations enable the learner to determine whether or not something belongs to a category and therefore he can, without error, assign to that thing all the other generalizations which are common to that category.

If this sounds complicated, let's look at a simpler example of generalizations about fish. Fish live in water, have tails and fins, "breathe" with gills, have an internal skeleton, scales, eyes, etc. If a child knows these generalizations, he can transfer them to any fish regardless of whether he has ever seen it or heard about it before. These generalizations, however, will not help him determine whether or not something *is* a fish. If an unknown animal has scales he could erroneously assume it was a fish when in reality it was a reptile. As a result, there would be negative transfer of his knowledge about fish.

To correctly assign to the new animal all the generalizations related to fish, he would need to know that the scaly animal possessed the critical attribute which verified it was a fish. (Use gills throughout its life cycle.)

It is important that we teach which generalizations are common to a group or category and which of those generalizations identify the critical attribute which makes the category what it is.

All of the following generalizations about mammals are valid so they should be learned. Which would you teach as the critical attribute so a learner would be able to know for sure that he was correct in transferring his previous knowledge to a new animal?

a. Mammals are warm blooded. . . . . Turn to page 80, top

b. Mammals have mammary glands. . . . . . Turn to page 80, bottom

c. Mammals bear their young alive. . . . . Turn to page 81, top

d. Mammals breathe air. . . . . Turn to page 81, bottom

a. You said that warm blooded is a critical attribute of mammals.

It's a valid generalization but it also applies to birds and will not discriminate between the two categories. Turn back to the question on page 79 and select the attribute which only mammals possess.

b. You said having mammary glands is a critical attribute of mammals.

Right you are! Because that is a critical attribute, it gives the category its name. Although there may be more than one critical attribute, knowing that a new animal has mammary glands enables the learner to transfer correctly everything he knows about the category. He also can correctly differentiate penguins, whales, seals, porpoises, and dolphins and assign (transfer) the appropriate generalizations. Turn to page 82 for another example of teaching generalizations and critical attributes.

c. You said bearing their young alive is a critical attribute.

In a way you're right. However, in some reptiles the egg hatches within the mother and the young emerge alive. Consequently, it would be possible to erroneously assign to that reptile all the characteristics of mammals. We included this answer to alert you to the dangers of any possible misperceptions or misconceptions of a generalization (i.e., birds have wings—a bat seems to have them and a penguin doesn't). Turn back to the question on page 79 and select the answer which would eliminate any possibility of error.

d. You said breathing air is a critical attribute.

We don't believe you did. If you're reading this it's only to see what we have to say which is that breathing air is a correct generalization about mammals but also applies to many other categories. Turn back to the question on page 79 so your degree of learning of the correct answer will transfer to your future teaching.

Another example of identification of the essential and unvarying element which "makes a situation what it is" is the attribute which distinguishes tattling from reporting. All of us wish to discourage "tattletales" yet we wish to encourage the reporting of dangerous or emergency situations. What is the key element that discriminates the desirable from the undesirable behavior? We teach youngsters that they shouldn't tell us every time John bothers Mary or Bill takes an extra piece of paper. We teach them they should report it if that same John threatens Mary with a knife or Bill takes something from another child's purse. What's the difference? Small wonder we have problems, for it is a difficult question to answer. Take a minute now to jot down what you think is the critical discriminator between tattling and reporting.

_____

_____

_____

_____

_____

_____

_____

_____

_____

_____

_____

If we pursue our quest to make explicit and teach the essential quality that distinguishes a tattletale from a model citizen, we will find that critical element exists not in the act but only in the motives of the tattler or reporter. A citizen who calls the police when he sees someone entering a window of his neighbor's house is reporting. His motive is to protect his neighbor, not to get a thief in trouble. That thief's former friend who "rats" on him and calls the police is not motivated to help the victim, he is getting his former associate in trouble. The stool pigeon is not attempting to help society, he is endeavoring to get someone in trouble or save his own skin. The victim of an extortion racket or blackmailer is probably not tattling but is attempting to help society even though he is taking a risk himself.

Because the essential element that distinguishes tattling from reporting is motivational, only the person who is doing it knows (and sometimes he doesn't) whether his action is noble or ignoble. Consequently, in school we need to teach for a student's examination of his motives and constantly refocus students on this essential discriminator. We need to ask, "Are you telling me to help or to get him in trouble?" followed by "How will that help?" and, "What do you want me to do to help him rather than get him in trouble?" These questions are important teaching stimuli so understanding from past learning about motives transfers to present behavior. It is important to remember that verbalizing (but not "parroting") results in an increase in transfer power when making discriminations.

Generalizations that are rules.

Transfer is always enhanced when the learner works out rules (generalizations) for what he's doing and makes those rules explicit. Those rules should (1) cover many examples, (2) have few exceptions, and (3) be easy to learn.

Try to work out the rule (if you don't already know it) for when to double the final consonant of a verb before adding "ed" or "ing."

walk	walked	walking
commit	committed	committing
trap	trapped	trapping
flop	flopped	flopping
climb	climbed	climbing
nab	nabbed	nabbing
bang	banged	banging
wag	wagged	wagging

Now test your ability to make your generalization explicit by writing the rule. The rule for doubling consonants when adding "ed" or "ing" is:

_____

_____

_____

If you are having trouble finding the rule, look at the letter just before the final consonant. (This is an example of guided discovery. We are not telling you the answer but we are focusing you on the key discriminator.)

Now what is your rule?_____

_____

_____

To the next page.

You probably have discovered that the final consonant is always preceded by a vowel when you double it before adding the suffix, Now look at these words and see if you can sharpen your rule:

saw	sawed	sawing
play	played	playing
float	floated	floating
look	looked	looking

Modify your rule so these words do not become exceptions.

_____

_____

_____

Turn to the next page.

You probably have modified your rule to "whenever the final consonant is preceded by a simple (short) vowel." You now have identified and labeled the key discriminator of a powerful generalization which should transfer to future spelling.

The learning of a generalization provides such powerful transfer that we have to place particular focus on any exceptions to that generalization to prevent that learning from transferring when it is inappropriate.

A youngster who has learned the generalization of the addition of "ed" to denote past tense of a verb is apt to have "comed to school." The "er" of bigger, shorter, and greener can be transferred to "gooder." Following what we have learned in this book we would teach the generalization and achieve an adequate degree of learning before we deliberately introduced the exceptions to that rule. *Teaching a rule and exceptions at the same time makes it more difficult for the student to perceive the generalization.*

Now if we practice what we are preaching about generalizations, we should identify and label those critical generalizations about "teaching generalizations to students" so you will focus on those critical attributes and transfer them to your teaching when you are encouraging your students to develop generalizations. (If you understood that sentence you are well on your way.)

First, we will list the generalizations about "how to teach generalizations" and then give teaching examples for each. Why don't we let you discover them for yourself instead of reading our list? Because, if it has taken psychologists years to do so, it is highly unlikely you will accomplish it in a few minutes. Besides, we wish to direct your energy to the more important discovery of how you can apply those generalizations in your classroom. That knowledge does not exist in a list that we can present to you.

The building of powerful transfer potential from a generalization begins with (a) the identification and *understanding* of key elements, major points or discriminators, important features or ideas, and processes from which the generalization is derived. (b) Next, the generalization must be successfully applied by your students to highly similar situations. (c) Only after such practice in application to similar situations can most students apply the generalization to situations which vary more and more from the original situation. (d) At this point a student should be able to generate additional examples where the generalization is applicable as well as situations where it is not. (e) Finally, the student is exposed to widely varying situations including some where the principle is not relevant so the learner will develop facility in its application but also become aware of the limitations of the generalization and realize that, inappropriately applied, it can lead to error.

Now let's do what we are telling you to do and translate this set of generalizations about *transfer through generalizations* including something you recognize as *similar* to teaching situations you have encountered so you will *learn those generalizations well* and *associate* them with lessons. Then what you learn in this book should transfer into your teaching behavior.

We'll use the example of teaching students to differentiate fact from opinion. We have selected this example because it is more apt to have been encountered in the past by readers of this book than if we selected an example which was relevant only for a certain content area such as science or math or physical education. In this way we'll be utilizing transfer from your past experience to facilitate present learning. We'll begin with the first step of identifying the key discriminators or generalizations which differentiate fact from opinion. What do you think they are?

If you want to increase your own learning through verbalization (and incidentally check to see what you've learned), stop reading for a minute and jot them down.

The critical discriminators between fact and opinion are:

_____

_____

_____

Turn to the next page.

What *is* the difference between fact and opinion?

"A fact is true" you may say. But an opinion also may be true and some "facts" later turn out to be false. We used to state as fact that what went up had to come down and a man on the moon was a myth. Consequently, "true" and "false" are *not* the essential discriminators of fact and opinion. We'll bet that before now, many of you had never made explicit the difference and just assumed "a fact is a fact and an opinion is what some people believe or think." Yet many people believe the "facts" and think they are facts. It's not easy, is it?

One of the reasons learners become confused is that often the teacher is "fuzzy" in identification of those key elements which signal a situation to be what it is. If the learner is to "discover" them so he develops the mental set to always be on the lookout for critical elements and generalizations (a set we highly endorse!), then the teacher should think it through carefully so the students' discovery can be made more productive and valid by skilled teacher guidance as well as have transfer propulsion from verbal labeling. Let's see how we would develop the steps we listed in teaching a generalization about fact and opinion.

a. Identification and understanding of key elements

While we are not attempting to develop a precise definition, we could utilize the generalization that a fact is something to which authorities in that field or area would agree and no evidence is known that would impeach it. An opinion could be a belief about something in a field or area where evidence may exist to support differing beliefs.

b. Applying the generalization to highly similar situations

Skillful teaching would imply that we begin teaching application of this generalization with examples where the distinguishing elements are obvious and within the previous experience of the learner so we can get a "boost" from positive transfer. John is a boy vs. John is the nicest boy. Mary is wearing a sweater vs. Mary is wearing the prettiest sweater.

c. Applying the generalization to situations that vary

Only after students can successfully label noncontroversial examples would we move to examples that varied more such as: "It happened at 7 a.m. It was early in the morning," and "We are in the 8th grade. Ours is the best class."

d. *Students generate examples*

At this point students should be encouraged to generate their own examples and practice transferring the generalization about fact and opinion to new situations. In each discrimination they should make explicit the key element. "My example is, 'Bill is the best ball player!' It's an opinion because other people who know just as much as I do think Tom is better," or "Ralph is the best violin player in the school." That's a fact because the orchestra tryouts were judged by musicians and they all agreed." Careful monitoring by the teacher, as well as by other students should minimize erroneous application. Such generation of examples emphasizes the presence of a continuum rather than discrete positions. This in itself is important for it will help students transfer the generalization, "You can't always be sure" and leads to the 5th step.

e. *Students become aware of the limitations of the generalization*

Finally, when appropriate skills are established, the student will transfer his ability to discriminate fact from opinion to such statements as "Some people believe in reincarnation," and "It is a fact that Mary says she prefers hamburgers but she always orders tuna sandwiches" or "Experts are of the opinion that the painting is a Rembrandt."

Obviously, these examples are not cited to teach the difference between fact and opinion but to assist you in transferring your knowledge about teaching generalizations into lesson plans and classroom practice. It becomes increasingly apparent that teaching to achieve the development of generalizations with their tremendous potential for transfer takes the highest type of professional competence.

5. Labeling the generalization being used.

Language is such a powerful variable in transfer that after they have had appropriate experience, student and/or teacher should verbally label a similarity, association, or critical factor which signals the appropriateness of a past learning to a new situation. This generalization is true even for disadvantaged learners with a language deficit. Learners need practice (but *not* parroting) with, "I'm reporting because_____" or "It's not a mammal because_____." Reinforcing a student's use of the correct discriminator will increase such transfer and help students learn more effectively. Words are records of generalizations and their use implies the power to apply to new experience the established classifications expressed in language.

We are identifying and labeling this critical generalization about "*labeling*" so it will transfer to your future teaching. It is essential that we focus on and *label the relevant* rather than irrelevant dimensions of a learning situation. If we transfer this generalization to our teaching, we will remove all the clutter of extraneous detail and emphasize those aspects which present the key concepts or unvarying elements of a learning. Consequently, beware of "running off at the mouth" and introducing a lot of possibly interesting but extraneous and therefore interfering detail ("now there are certain mammals that have_____" or "in some cases of fact and opinion we can _____") while you are trying to teach the basic concept. Remember exceptions and less obvious examples come *after* the generalization is well learned. Practice should be on meaningful material already mastered, done with full attention, and checked for accuracy.

Applications of this admonition are that we teach the big ideas of history, not have students expend their learning effort on a list of names and dates of battles; that we focus on the message and style of literature, not insist on memorized passages or trivia related to the author; that in teacher education we stress and label the factors that promote learning rather than the specifics of particular methods or "how to" recipes.

CHAPTER VI
SUMMARY

Now let's see how well this book has taught for transfer. Can you identify and verbally label the essential and invariant generalizations which will enable you to plan to "Teach for Transfer"?

1. Transfer is important because _____

_____

_____

_____

2. The four categories of factors which encourage transfer are:

    a. _____

    b. _____

    c. _____

    d. _____

3. Verbalizing the critical element which triggers appropriate transfer is desirable because

_____

_____

_____

4. The most important factor promoting transfer (not because it is more powerful but because it is more subject to instructional control) is

_____

_____

_____

Now check your answers with the generalizations on the next page.

1. Transfer is important because it is the heart and core of problem solving, creative thinking, and all other higher mental processes as well as inventions and artistic products. It provides a source of real economy in time and energy in learning.

2. The four categories of factors which encourage transfer are:

   a. Similarity of environment, actions, and feelings.

   b. Association of two learnings.

   c. Adequate degree of the original learning.

   d. Identification and labeling of the critical and invariant properties or generalizations that make a situation what it is.

3. Verbalizing the critical element which triggers transfer is desirable because the act of making explicit and labeling (1) focuses the learner on the critical element rather than an unimportant one and (2) increases the conscious recognition of that element in a new situation.

4. The most important factor promoting transfer (not because it is more powerful but because it is more subject to instructional control) is the identification of those critical and unvarying elements, attributes and generalizations which signal that something is what it is, so positive transfer will take place and inappropriate transfer will not occur. To achieve this skill we should teach (1) categorization, (2) identification of critical attributes, (3) predifferentiation skills, (4) generalizations.

Now turn back to your original answers on page 8 and see what you have learned by reading this book. Only by learning the generalizations about transfer and labeling those generalizations can you *consciously, appropriately and systematically* transfer that learning into your teaching. Now that you know that your instructional approach is more significant than your students *per se* you will realize that *it is not sufficient for learners to merely understand the meaning of concepts and generalizations. They must be able to apply this learning productively outside the classroom setting.* You, as their teacher, should develop strategies so they acquire and use knowledge to implement the problem-solving and creative process rather than acquiring knowledge as an end product.

A series of generalizations that should guide you and your students (they should learn to use these also) are:

1. Always look for knowledge in past experiences that will propel present learning.

2. Identify and label the *similarities* of the two learnings which make transfer from one appropriate to the other.

3. Use appropriate *associations* from the past and develop productive present associations.

4. Elicit the appropriate *set to perform*.

5. Make sure learning is achieved to an *appropriate degree*.

6. Identify and *label the key discriminators* that make a situation what it *is*.

7. *Practice* transfer. Tranfer itself may be made to transfer and is a critical attribute of "learning how to learn."

In this book you have used the *mode of attack* of using psychological theory to solve learning and behavior problems so it will transfer to your teaching behavior. To accomplish this, in presenting psychological theory, we have made the situations described in this book as *similar* as possible to those you encounter in the classroom. We presented teaching problems and generalizations from theory together so you will form an *association* that will transfer those generalizations to your plans and actions for solution of future problems. If we have made this book meaningful, the content will be *well learned* and therefore more apt to transfer appropriately. Finally, by focusing on the *labeling generalizations* as well as *identifying the critical elements* in theory and practice situations you should forever abandon the "what in the world will I do now?" stance and apply psychological theory to a learning situation, consciously identifying those critical invariant elements or attributes which make such transfer valid. The increase in students' learning from your utilization of possibilities for transfer will really amaze you.

Remember, *all teaching should be for transfer*. In addition to direct facilitation of learning, broad transfer effects, such as confidence in oneself as a learner and general approach to learning, are retained long after the details of a practiced task are forgotten. Teaching for transfer should be your ultimate professional goal for it synthesizes the science of human learning and the artistry of the true professional.